1

I. Introduction

The U.S. petroleum industry has undergone substantial restructuring since the mid 1990's. Among the major industry events were the creation of the Shell-Texaco and Marathon-Ashland joint ventures, and the BP-Amoco, Exxon-Mobil, BP-ARCO, Chevron-Texaco, and Phillips-Conoco mergers. Critics of the industry contend that the increase in concentration from these transactions has led to higher prices. Some government officials have called for a moratorium on petroleum mergers.[2] In contrast, the industry contends that these mergers have led to considerable costs savings. Before the Exxon-Mobil merger was completed the companies predicted that they would save $2.8 billion a year in costs. Two years after the merger was completed Exxon-Mobil stated they had achieved $4.6 billion dollars a year in savings.[3]

Despite the size of the petroleum industry and the controversy surrounding petroleum mergers, there have been surprisingly few attempts to examine the effect of mergers on the price of gasoline.[4] The few papers examining petroleum mergers typically either estimate the effects of a large number of mergers in a single study, or only examine one level of the industry, typically wholesale (rack) pricing.[5] The conventional approaches taken to study petroleum

_____

[2]"I urge Congress to enact a moratorium of at least one year on any merger or acquisitions of any major oil refiner, supplier or retailer, including cross-sector mergers and acquisitions, while Congress, the FTC and the states work together to fashion a longer term remedy that helps restore competitive forces and tempers the market dominance wielded by the few industry giants." Testimony of Connecticut Attorney General Richard Blumenthal Before the Permanent Subcommittee on Investigations of the Senate Governmental Affairs Committee, May 2, 2002.

[3]ExxonMobil Corporation, *Investor and Media Meeting*, New York, Aug. 1, 2000, pp. 36-37.

[4] There have been attempts to indirectly look at merger effects by examining changes in concentration. (GAO, 1986) Simply using concentration as a proxy for merger effects is problematic on a number of theoretical and practical levels, e.g. the difficulty of defining markets correctly and controlling for endogenous market structure. (Evans et al., 1993)

[5]The most commonly examined wholesale price for gasoline is the rack price. The rack price is the price posted at the truck rack at a terminal for trucks loading branded or unbranded gasoline. The percentage of wholesale transactions taking place at the rack prices varies by geography and by firm.

mergers are problematic for two reasons. First, examining multiple mergers in a single study is a virtually untenable task. The creation of boutique fuel specifications to comply with environmental regulations has Balkanized gasoline distribution in the U.S.[6] Each region of the U.S. is subject to different idiosyncratic sources of price variation, such as supply outages, input price fluctuations, seasonal changes in marginal supply and formulation changes. In order to ascertain how prices changed as the result of a change in market structure, the researcher must control for all of these complicating factors. Second, researchers should be careful about measuring merger affects by examining wholesale (rack) prices alone. In any gasoline market, there are multiple wholesale prices being charged to gasoline retailers, only some of which are publicly observable.[7] In addition, because petroleum mergers often affect the vertical structure of a local gasoline market, any given transaction may affect the retail markup a retail outlet earns, while having little effect on the retail price of gasoline.[8]

For these reasons, in this study we examine one transaction, the refining and marketing joint venture of Marathon and Ashland to form Marathon Ashland Petroleum (MAP). The MAP transaction proceeded with no antitrust challenge or divestiture. Testimony by various participants before the Permanent Subcommittee on Investigations of the Senate Governmental Affairs Committee, on May 2, 2002 suggested that the increased concentration from this merger, and mergers in general, have led to higher or more volatile gasoline prices in the Midwest.[9] In

---

[6]Before the changes in gasoline specifications brought about by the Clean Air Act there was one gasoline specification in the country, now there are 18. Energy Information Administration, Petroleum Supply Monthly, April 1999.

[7]Also the relationship between these different wholesale prices may change, often in response to supply outages. For example, lessee dealer stations, a station owned by a major oil company leased by an independent marketer, pay a "dealer-tank-wagon" or DTW price which is typically higher than the posted rack price, but when refineries have supply problems, the DTW price is often less than the posted rack price.

[8]There are a number of theoretical models that demonstrate how mergers, both horizontal and vertical mergers may affect upstream (wholesale) but not downstream (retail) prices. For examples of these types of models see, Ordover et al., (1990) and Froeb et al., (2002).

[9]"Increased concentration in the refining and distribution segment of the industry has contributed to the exercise of market power by dominant industry actors to the detriment of

this paper we examine how the retail and wholesale prices of gasoline in arguably the most potentially problematic area, Louisville, Kentucky, changed as a result of the joint venture. We use the wholesale and retail price of gasoline in a number of cities as controls in estimating whether the retail or wholesale price of gasoline changed in Louisville as a result of the joint venture.

Retail gasoline prices in Louisville do not appear to increase as a result of the joint venture. These findings are robust when comparing the retail price in Louisville to three control markets. The wholesale (rack) prices of reformulated gasoline (RFG) increased 3-5 cents per gallon approximately 15 months after the transaction. This wholesale price (rack) effect, however, seem to be the result of a supply shock caused by St. Louis's switch to RFG rather than the joint venture. The difference in the retail and wholesale (rack) price changes demonstrates that it is crucial to examine both retail and wholesale pricing when measuring the price effects of a merger affecting gasoline markets. The finding that the wholesale price increase is not passed through at retail is somewhat surprising. In this market, it appears that retailers directly supplied by refiners, representing 30% of gasoline sales, did not experience a wholesale price increase in 1999. Apparently those stations facing the higher wholesale (rack price) were not able to pass through enough of the price increase to affect the average market price because of competition with stations directly supplied by refiners.[10]

The paper is organized as follows. The second section provides industry background and then describes the structure of the MAP joint venture. Section three reviews the methodologies used in merger retrospectives for various industries and those research papers that focus on

---

consumers." and "Although not as large as the mergers referenced above on a national scale, the most significant transactions in Michigan petroleum markets involve the merger of Marathon and Ashland Petroleum and then later Marathon Ashland Petroleum's acquisition of all the Ultramar Diamond Shamrock assets in the State." Testimony of the Michigan Attorney General Jennifer Granholm before the Permanent Subcommittee on Investigations of the Senate Governmental Affairs Committee, May 2, 2002.

[10]Competition from stations selling conventional gasoline which did not experience a wholesale price increase directly across the Ohio River in Indiana or in Kentucky, outside the RFG area, may also have limited the ability of rack supplied stations to pass thru the wholesale price increase.

potential price effects of petroleum mergers. The fourth section describes the data used in the analysis. The fifth and sixth sections discuss the results of the analysis and the interpretation of the results, and the last section discusses conclusions.

II. Industry Background and the Marathon/Ashland Transaction

A. Industry Background

Empirical analysis of gasoline pricing in the United States requires some familiarity with the institutional structure of the gasoline refining and distribution system that affect the pricing of gasoline. This section discusses the institutional structure that is of particular relevance for estimating the price effects of MAP. There are five main components of retail gasoline prices (costs): crude oil acquisition cost, refining costs, distribution and marketing costs, and taxes. The size and volatility of refining, wholesaling and marketing costs in different regions of the United States are affected by the myriad of gasoline formulations used in various regions and the multiple sources of supply to a given region. In addition to conventional gasoline, other fuel specifications exist which are designed to reduce emissions and air pollution. Such specifications are usually some form of oxygengenated or reformulated gasoline (RFG). The federal government has developed specifications for RFG, and there are different specifications for the North and South and some areas uses a different oxygenate, either MTBE (methyl tertiary-butyl ether) or ethanol. Some areas have their own formulations to satisfy federal clean air requirements without using RFG. These "boutique" gasoline formulations tend to cost less to produce, on average. However, in periods of supply disruption, e.g., a refinery outage, it can be difficult for refiners to ship gasoline to an affected region quickly because alternative supplies of that region's specific type of gasoline may not be readily available.

A city's source of gasoline supply varies significantly throughout the United States. The eastern half of the United States is linked by a network of pipelines and waterways which connect large refining areas in the Gulf Coast, the upper Midwest and the Northeast. While most regions of the country receive some of their gasoline from local refineries, the source of marginal supply varies across the U.S. and may change during the year. The Gulf Coast of the U.S.

(refineries in Texas and Louisiana) produces much more gasoline than it consumes, and ships gasoline to the Midwest and East Coast. The eastern region of the U.S. is a net importer of gasoline, with marginal supply coming from the Gulf via pipeline and from Canada, Europe and the Caribbean via ports around New York City. Most of the gasoline consumed in the upper Midwest, e.g., Illinois or Minnesota, is refined locally, but the region receives marginal supply from the Gulf.

Not only does the method of supply vary by geography, but vertical integration among levels of the petroleum industry- crude exploration, refining, wholesaling and marketing- vary by firm and geography as well. Some firms, such as Exxon-Mobil, are vertically integrated from the exploration and production of crude oil through refining, wholesaling and marketing. Other firms, such as Tesoro, concentrate on refining and marketing, and other firms concentrate on simply refining, such as Koch, or marketing, such as Sheetz or Racetrac.

Further complicating the vertical market structure in the industry, there are also different vertical relationships between the wholesale and retail levels of the industry.[11] A branded gasoline station, e.g. Exxon or Shell, may be owned and operated by an oil company (company op), owned by the oil company and leased to an independent operator (lessee dealer), or owned and operated by an independent operator (open dealer). It is important to note that each of these retail/wholesale vertical relationships results in a potentially different wholesale price. The company owned and operated station pays an unobserved transfer price for gasoline, the lessee dealer typically pays a dealer tank wagon price which can vary by station and which is difficult to observe, and the open dealer typically pays the rack price plus delivery and possibly a markup to the delivery firm which is somewhat observable. The percentage of branded stations of each vertical type varies dramatically by brand and geography.[12] While this is a very abbreviated summary of some important facts about the petroleum industry, it serves to outline those factors

---

[11]The vertical market structure is impacted in a number of states by divorcement regulations, restrictions on petroleum companies owning gasoline stations. See, Vita (2000) and Blass and Carlton (2001) for a description, and the estimated economic impact, of divorcement.

[12]For a more detailed description of the wholesale gasoline markets and DTW and rack pricing see Borenstein and Shepard (1994).

that affect the wholesale and retail price of gasoline. In particular, given the different relationships between suppliers and retailers, it is important to understand the vertical structure of local markets and the pricing at different levels when examining the potential effects of any consummated merger.

B. The Marathon-Ashland Joint Venture

The MAP joint venture affected both the wholesale and retail distribution of gasoline in the Midwest. This was one of the first major transactions in the most recent era of petroleum mergers and it caused significant changes in concentration. Many subsequent mergers did not cause important changes in concentration because of substantial divestitures required by regulators. In May of 1997, USX-Marathon and Ashland Inc, announced that they planned to combine their downstream operations into a refining and marketing company. The joint venture included 930,000 barrels per day of refining capacity at seven refineries, and 5,400 retail outlets. The joint venture was owned 62 percent by Marathon and 38 percent by Ashland. The refineries from Marathon were in Garyville, Louisiana, Robinson, Illinois, Texas City, Texas, and Detroit, Michigan. The refineries from Ashland were in Catlettsburg, Kentucky, St. Paul, Minnesota, and Canton, Ohio.

In addition, Marathon contributed 51 terminals and Ashland contributed 33 terminals. Marathon contributed 3,980 retail outlets in 17 states and Ashland contributed 1,420 retail outlets in 11 states. The combined firm has a retail presence in 20 states. Marathon also contributed 5,000 miles of pipelines to the joint venture (Platt's Oilgram News, May 16, 1997). Marathon and Ashland signed the definitive joint venture agreement in December 1997, and consummated the joint venture on January 1, 1998.

Marathon and Ashland acknowledged that the Federal Trade Commission (FTC) was reviewing the transaction and that they had received a second request for information. A Prudential Securities report in October of 1997 stated that Ashland had completed its FTC document request and anticipated approval in "four to six weeks." A December 1997 news story commented that the FTC had signed off on the merger and did not mandate any divestiture (Platt's Oilgram News, December 15, 1997). The FTC does not usually publicly acknowledge that it is conducting a particular merger investigation nor does it issue statements about closed investigations. There were no FTC announcements concerning the MAP joint venture.

There were three levels of the petroleum industry where anticompetitive effects were possible as a result of this merger: refining and the wholesale and retail distribution of gasoline in the area. Five of the joint venture's refineries were located in the Midwest, and two were located in the Gulf Coast (where the market was not concentrated). Gasoline consumed in the Midwest comes from refineries in the area and from pipelines and barges that shipped gasoline from the Gulf Coast to the Midwest. While Marathon and Ashland competed throughout the Midwest, given their respective refinery locations, Ashland had a much larger presence in the eastern and northwestern portions of the Midwest and Marathon had a larger market presence in the central portion of Midwest.

At the wholesale level, Marathon or Ashland were among the top four suppliers in nine states in 1996 and 1997, according to Department of Energy, Energy Information Administration data. These nine states were Kentucky, Ohio, West Virginia, Indiana, Illinois, Michigan, Minnesota, South Carolina, and North Dakota. There was only one state, Kentucky, where both Marathon and Ashland were among the top four wholesale suppliers. The wholesale HHI, sum of squared market shares, for Kentucky (the narrowest region for which we can calculate an HHI with publicly available data) increased by about 800 points from 1477 in 1997 to 2263 in 1998.[13,14]

Figure 1 shows the Marathon and Ashland refineries in the central Midwest as well as the other refineries and pipelines in the area where the largest wholesale overlap occurred. Not surprisingly, like the wholesale overlaps, the highest retail market shares from the joint venture were in Kentucky (26%), Ohio (26%) and Indiana (27%). In Indiana almost the entire market share was from Marathon. In the other two states, Kentucky and Ohio, the HHI increased by

---

[13]Department of Energy, Energy Information Administration, Petroleum Supply Annual, 1997-1998.

[14]Implicit in this calculation is the assumption that the state of Kentucky is a market. For the region we study, Louisville, the number of firms posting a rack price for conventional gasoline went from eight to seven and for RFG from four to three.

over 250 points to 1500 to 1600 range. These retail market shares are based on sales of gasoline by brand. Since some of the branded stations are independently owned and could switch brands, these market shares overstate the concentration.

Given the concentration measures, both at wholesale and at retail, and the location of the refineries, Kentucky appears to be the area most likely place to experience an anticompetitive effect from the MAP joint venture. We are agnostic as to whether the possible anticompetitive problem may be at the refining, wholesaling or retailing level.

Within Kentucky, we concentrate our analysis on Louisville for a number of reasons. First, it is the largest major metropolitan area in Kentucky.[15] Second, Louisville is directly between the two refineries (Robinson and Cattletsburg), see Figure 1, and both Marathon and Ashland had a large retail and wholesale presence. Third, Louisville uses RFG, which makes arbitrage from nearby regions (that use conventional gasoline) more difficult.[16] In other words, while in most parts of the Midwest one or the other of the firms had a significant presence pre-joint venture, Louisville is the place where they most directly overlapped and where each had a major presence.

III. Literature Review

This section reviews the methodology used in studies that use pre- and post-merger pricing data to estimate merger effects and the results of papers that examine the effects of petroleum mergers. While many papers discuss merger effects, there is not a large literature on the estimated price effects of mergers outside of historically regulated industries, e.g., banking,

---

[15]See Figure II for a map of the Louisville MSA and the gasoline station locations.

[16]We also analyzed conventional gasoline prices at the Louisville rack and at retail in the area surrounding the RFG area in Louisville relative to the control cities. There was no change in the price of conventional gasoline at the Louisville rack or in the surrounding retail areas. Figure VII shows the price of conventional gasoline at the Louisville rack relative the Chicago rack. There is no change in the price of conventional gasoline.

health care, and airlines.[17] Most merger event studies that examine product prices before and after a merger use one of three types of reduced form regressions.

In the first type of regression (*see* Barton and Sherman (1984) and Kim and Singal (1993)), the price of the product affected by the merger is compared to the price of a product that faces similar demand and cost conditions but is unaffected by the merger. Specifically, the price of the product of the merged firm is regressed on the price of the control product(s) and controls for time or seasonality and a merger dummy variable. In the second type of regression (*see* Schumann *et al.*, (1992) and (1997)), the price of the merged firm's product (or market price) is regressed on demand and supply/cost shifters plus a merger dummy. A third approach combines elements of both approaches. In their study of a hospital merger, Vita and Sacher (2001) examine the price of the merged firm relative to the price of a control group of firms unaffected by the merger that should be affected by the same demand and supply factors. They then regressed these relative prices on relative demand shifters, relative cost shifters, and the merger event to gauge the effect of the merger.

The second approach, which relies completely on demand and supply variables, is problematic in this case. There are few variables that are available on a weekly or monthly basis at the city level to help explain wholesale or retail gasoline price variation. The most promising approach for gasoline markets is the control city approach with possibly additional variables to check for marginal supply changes. These marginal supply changes are likely seasonal, caused by peak capacity of pipelines or refineries.

One published paper and three recent working papers have estimated merger effects in gasoline markets by either calculating the actual effect of consummated petroleum mergers on gasoline prices or simulating the projected price effects from proposed mergers that were not actually consummated.[18] These papers are representative of the wide range of the methodologies

---

[17]For a review of the literature on the multitude of methodologies used in examining the effects of mergers, including those papers that attempt to directly estimate the price effects see, Pautler (2003).

[18]In addition to the recent working papers discussed in the text, a government report by the U.S. General Accounting Office (GAO, 1986) examined gasoline prices from the time period

used in merger retrospectives, single event studies, a cross-section of multiple mergers and simulations of mergers with estimated parameters.

Hastings (2004) uses an event study methodology to examine how changes in retail gasoline prices might be attributed to differing vertical contracts and brand affiliations. This paper examines the price effects of ARCO's 1997 long term lease of 260 service stations from Thrifty, an unbranded and unintegrated retailer; that is, prior to the acquisition Thrifty purchased all of its gasoline from refining firms. ARCO was a major branded marketer which was also integrated into refining and crude production. The affected stations were primarily in Los Angeles and San Diego and increased ARCO's already considerable retail presence in these areas. About two thirds of the Thrifty stations were converted to company-operated ARCO sites while the others were converted to ARCO lessee-dealer or independently-owned ARCO stations. Using station level retail prices and controlling for other factors, Hastings finds that gasoline prices at nearby, competing stations increased (relative to a control group of stations not having a nearby Thrifty outlet) by about 5 cents per gallon, after the conversion of the Thirty station to ARCO. The estimated impact on competitors' prices did not differ if the rebranded station became an ARCO company operated station or an ARCO lessee dealer station.[19]

Hastings and Gilbert (2002) use an event study of the 1997 Tosco/Unocal Transaction to examine the impact of vertical market structure on gasoline prices.[20] Tosco purchased three

---

surrounding Texaco's purchase of Getty and Chevron's purchase of Gulf. Having only limited post-merger data, GAO did not directly estimate the price effects of the two mergers. Instead it estimated a wholesale price- concentration relationship and inferred a price increase resulting from a change in concentration. Since the FTC-required divestitures prevented concentration increases where the merger guidelines thresholds would have been exceeded and because the correlation between HHI and wholesale price appeared small, the GAO concluded that the two mergers "would have had only a small effect on wholesale gasoline prices." The report concluded that supply changes other than the mergers were primarily responsible for the observed increase in prices in 1985.

[19] Other research papers have found that company operated stations have, on average, lower prices than lessee dealers. See Shepard (1993) and Barron and Umbeck (1984).

[20] In the paper there is also a price-concentration regression looking at the relationship between both vertical and horizontal market structure and the wholesale price of unbranded gasoline in metropolitan areas in the Western United States. The authors find that the difference between

California refineries along with 1,100 gasoline stations and related terminals and transportation assets from Unocal. Tosco owned two refineries on the West Coast, one in California and one in Washington, but had a limited retail presence in California. Their analysis examines whether Tosco raised rivals' costs by increasing the price of unbranded gasoline after it acquired Unocal's West Coast assets. The statistical results show a positive relationship between Tosco's price of unbranded gasoline and the increase in vertical integration caused by the purchase of Unocal assets by Tosco. The size of the estimated effect depends on the change in vertical integration caused by the merger. For example, if in a given city 20 percent of the acquired (Unocal) retail outlets were within a mile of the an independent (unbranded) competitor, Tosco raised its unbranded wholesale price in that city by 0.7 cents per gallon. While the paper shows that Tosco/Unocal raised the wholesale price of unbranded gasoline, the paper does not examine what happened to retail prices. Thus, while this paper provides evidence that the change in market structure affected Tosco's wholesale prices, it is unclear that consumers were made worse off as a result of the transaction.

Chouinard and Perloff (2001) examine gasoline price changes over time and differences in prices among geographic areas using monthly state-level retail and wholesale (rack) prices for the period between January 1989 and June 1997. They estimate separate regressions for the determinants of retail prices and wholesale prices. Their analysis uses a state level fixed-effect specification. To isolate the effect of horizontal mergers and divestitures, Chouinard and Perloff include dummy variables for the presence of a refinery or retail merger among their explanatory variables in their wholesale and retail price regressions. A merger is assumed to affect state retail and wholesale prices from the date it is completed to the end of the data set in June 1997. A total of 35 mergers were included in the analysis with 27 at the retail level and eight at the refinery level. Most mergers yielded statistically insignificant impacts. Nine of 27 retail mergers and three of the eight refinery mergers showed a statistically significant retail price effect; only

unbranded wholesale gasoline prices and crude prices is positively correlated with a measure of vertical integration. The authors point out that a positive statistical correlation between vertical integration and price should not be interpreted as necessarily demonstrating causality.

six of the 27 retail mergers and three of eight refinery mergers showed a statistically significant price effect on wholesale prices.

Among the mergers that showed a statistically significant price effect, the direction of estimated price effects were mixed. Retail mergers and refinery mergers were shown to both increase and decrease state-level prices. The same was true for wholesale prices as well: retail and refinery mergers were associated with both higher and lower wholesale prices. The estimated average effects are very small, with retail mergers leading to a 0.01 cents per gallon increase in retail prices and a 0.15 cent per gallon increase in the wholesale price. The overall effect of wholesale mergers was a 0.11 decrease in the average retail price and a 0.13 cent per gallon increase in the wholesale price. There were no large national or regional mergers that took place during the time period analyzed in this paper. While the paper does not list all the mergers that are considered (35), the four it does list are fairly small and unlikely to have a sizeable effect on concentration.[21]

Manusazak (2002) simulates the effect of oil mergers using a structural oligopoly model in the petroleum industry that incorporates the divisions between the upstream producers and the downstream retailers. The downstream, retail, sector is modeled as imperfectly competitive due to product differentiation primarily based on location. The upstream, wholesale, level of the model assumes that these firms set prices to maximize profits given the level of competition in the retail sector.

The model uses data on the retail price and quantity of gasoline along with attributes about the specific gasoline stations to estimate the demand model and the retail and wholesale pricing equations. The estimated model's parameters are used to simulate upstream petroleum mergers in Hawaii including the 1997 Equilon joint venture that would have combined Texaco

---

[21]The merger with the largest estimated price increase, 5 cents per gallon in the price of gasoline, Midway Oil's purchase of Kerr-McGee Rio Grande Valley, was reported to affect Arizona when the sale was 10 gasoline stations in Texas. The largest estimated wholesale effect, a 5.8 cent per gallon increase, was reported for Signal Hill Petroleum's 1992 purchase of a Fletcher Oil refinery. This was a 30 thousand barrel per day plant which was closed when Signal Hill backed out of the purchase. However, the closure of this refinery would likely not have had this large of an effect on the price of gasoline in California given its small size.

and Shell marketing assets in the state. Manuszak finds that there would have been anticompetitive effects if this joint venture had been completed as originally proposed. In fact, the FTC required Texaco to divest its Hawaiian assets before allowing the joint venture to proceed. The author concludes the FTC concerns were warranted but that the dead weight loss would have been relatively small due to the inelastic demand for gasoline. The simulated price effect of any two firms on Maui merging was between 2 and 3 cents per gallon.

Each of these studies has used a slightly different methodology but ultimately all examine the possible price effects of mergers comparing a pre- and post-merger period either through an event study or simulation. The effects found in these studies run the gamut from small price decreases to sizeable price increases. These studies do point out a number of issues that must be addressed in a merger retrospective. It is important to examine both wholesale and retail pricing post merger since the vertical and horizontal competition may have been affected. The event study, dummy variable approach, without control prices, is problematic because few market-specific high-frequency supply and demand variables for gasoline are available. In addition, examining multiple mergers using a panel data approach can be difficult without carefully controlling for each region's supply situation. Given these issues, we focus our attention on a measuring the price effect of a single petroleum merger affecting one market at both the wholesale and retail level and compare prices in the affected market with other markets that face similar supply and demand conditions but should be unaffected by the merger.

IV. Data and Methodology

The goal of this study is to determine how, if at all, prices changed in the Louisville wholesale and retail gasoline markets as a result of the MAP joint venture. While it is relatively straightforward to determine how prices changed following the joint venture, it is much more difficult to determine how prices changed relative to the "but-for" world where no joint venture took place. Specifically, before attributing any price effect to the combination of assets, we must control for exogenous changes in supply and demand that may have affected price. The method we use to control for changes other than the joint venture is to measure gasoline prices in

Louisville relative to other markets unaffected by the merger facing similar supply and demand conditions.

Many factors specific to gasoline markets complicate this approach. First, the specification of gasoline used in Louisville is different from that used in other nearby markets. This factor limits our comparison of Louisville gasoline markets to three regions using RFG (Chicago, Houston, and stations in the Northern Virginia suburbs of Washington, D.C.). However, even within these three regions there are differences in the fuel specification. Second, the physical distance (and means of supply) between cities causes some cities to be better controls for the "but-for" world than others. Third, all gasoline markets are linked at some level. Changes in prices, particularly large changes in price, in one market likely manifest themselves in nearby markets over some time period. Thus, strictly speaking, it is very difficult to argue that prices in a control city are completely exogenous from those prices being studied. Fourth, a number of factors could potentially complicate the measure of "price" in gasoline markets. There are two differences we focus on here: the different quality grades of gasoline (regular and premium) and the differences in branded and unbranded gasoline pricing. In the remainder of this section we describe the various methods we use to examine how the relative price in Louisville changed following the acquisition.

The Kentucky portion of the Louisville metropolitan area was the only region within a significant distance using RFG, other than the Kentucky suburbs of Cincinnati which was also affected by the transaction, in the time period immediately surrounding the joint venture. In the mid 1990's there was only one other area, Chicago/Milwaukee, in the Midwest that used RFG.

Gasoline prices in Chicago were arguably the best control price available for this study. While Marathon was a small participant in the (very large) Chicago market, Ashland was not present. Consequently, Marathon was unlikely to have much ability to significantly affect prices in Chicago. Chicago and Louisville faced similar demand conditions. Because both cities are in the same region of the country, both face similar demand shocks, e.g., experience similar weather in a given season. Both cities also received marginal supply from the Gulf, and both were a similar distance from the Gulf. Louisville's conventional gasoline and RFG comes from local refineries as well as from the Gulf. Chicago receives conventional gasoline from the Gulf but is self-sufficient in RFG with ethanol production during this period. (Bulow et al. (2003)) Hence, broad costs shocks should be passed through in a similar manner. Marathon also owned a refinery (in Robinson, Illinois) that was connected to both Chicago and Louisville via a pipeline. Through this pipeline Marathon could have shifted supply from Louisville (where it may have gained market power following the joint venture) to Chicago where it could have likely sold excess supply while having little impact on price.

There were two key drawbacks to using Chicago as a control city. The first was that Chicago only used RFG with ethanol. Louisville used both RFG made with ethanol and MTBE. In our data, we were able to consistently observe only the wholesale price for RFG in Louisville sold with MTBE. For this reason, our empirical analysis uses the wholesale price of RFG with MTBE in Louisville. Thus, comparisons between wholesale gasoline prices in Chicago and Louisville compared slightly different types of gasoline.[22] The wholesale prices of RFG made with MTBE and ethanol sold in Louisville appear to have a virtually constant differential (with one exception) during our time period; that is, the relative price of the two types of RFG in Louisville do not appear to change over time. For this reason, we do not believe our results would change if we had a complete wholesale price series on wholesale RFG made with ethanol. At retail, it was not possible to determine which stations in Louisville sold RFG made with MTBE or ethanol. Thus, when examining relative differences in *retail* prices we compared an (unknown) mix of ethanol and MTBE RFG prices in Louisville to ethanol prices in Chicago. Second, while the marginal supply to both Chicago and Louisville was the Gulf, the method of shipment was different. If, for some reason, either the pipeline serving Chicago were out of service or something affected the shipment of gasoline into Louisville by barge, then the relative price between the two cities might have diverged.[23]

---

[22]While the gasoline differs between the two cities, the distinction between conventional gasoline and RFG is much greater; that is, RFG made with ethanol is a much closer supply-side substitute than conventional gasoline.

[23]With the exception of a major barge accident that limited shipments into Louisville for a few days in August 1999, we are unaware of any shocks to the pipeline that served Chicago or the barges that served Louisville during our time period.

The remaining controls were the prices of gasoline in Houston and the Northern Virginia suburbs of Washington, D.C. Both of these regions used RFG, although the specification was somewhat different than that used in Chicago and Louisville.[24] Houston pricing is a good control since it is located in the center of the Gulf refining region which was a net exporter of gasoline to the rest of the country. Thus, the Houston price of gasoline was likely a good measure of the "spot" price of RFG gasoline in the U.S. Northern Virginia, while quite distant from Louisville, had the same marginal source of supply as Louisville. Neither Houston or Northern Virginia were affected by the combination of Marathon and Ashland. The remainder of cities using RFG in the U.S. in the time period immediately preceding and following the merger faced very different supply and demand conditions and did not make good control cities.[25]

Following similar studies using the event study methodology, we focus on a time period long enough to allow firms to change their behavior to take advantage of any increased market power or efficiencies resulting from the joint venture, but short enough that changes in market conditions unrelated to the joint venture do not swamp the effects we are interested in measuring. A priori, we do not know how long firms need to determine how to optimally change their output and pricing decisions. One might expect a firm could relatively quickly exploit its market power following a merger if it understood the structure of demand and supply. Alternatively, a significant amount of time may be required for firms involved in complicated refining processes to begin capturing the benefits of integration.[26] For these reasons, we analyze a fairly narrow window prior to the joint-venture, January 1, 1998, one year, to measure the pre-joint venture competitive environment, and examine two years of data following the joint venture. In the

---

[24]Houston and Northern Virginia use the "southern" specification of RFG made with MTBE. Louisville and Chicago use the "northern" specification.

[25] For example, the cities in the Northeast that used RFG, e.g., New York and Boston, received marginal supplies from Europe or the Caribbean via ports in New York and New Jersey in addition to the Gulf. Similarly, areas in California that used RFG have a very different specification of gasoline. St. Louis began using RFG June 1, 1999, after the transaction took place, and cannot be used as a control city in our study.

[26]Efficiencies make take a number of years to be realized. See, e.g., Focarelli and Panetta (2003).

empirical analysis, we calculate price effects separately comparing the pre-joint venture state of the world to the year directly following the joint venture (1998) and the second year following the joint venture (1999). The data used in the analysis this covers the time period from January 1st, 1997 through December 31, 1999. We do not examine data more than two years after the joint venture because of the major supply shocks affecting the price of gasoline in the Midwest in 2000 and 2001.[27]

Our price data comes from the Oil Price Information Service (OPIS). OPIS collects data on retail and wholesale prices in a large number of markets in the U.S. OPIS's wholesale price data consists of daily refiner-specific price quotes for different grades of gasoline (regular, mid-grade, or premium), both branded and unbranded, in roughly 360 markets in the United States.[28] OPIS also sells retail price data. The data are generated from a sample of retail outlets that accept fleet cards.[29] OPIS records the actual transaction price charged at the station on a given day. While the gasoline pricing data from OPIS is among the best available, there are two potentially important issues to recognize when using this data. First, a price is only recorded for a specific station, if a purchase is made at that station; that is, if no one with a fleet card purchases gasoline at a station no price is recorded for that station on that day. In our data *no* single station has a complete time series of prices, and many stations have very few price quotes (e.g., fewer than one a week). For this reason, stations that sell more gasoline are more likely to be sampled on any given day. We cannot, however, determine how the sample scheme OPIS

---

[27] These shocks were the result of unanticipated refinery outages and difficulty in changing gasoline specifications. For this reason, it is difficult to view gasoline pricing in the Midwestern U.S. (including Louisville and Chicago) as being in equilibrium in 2000 and 2001. These problems in the gasoline markets have been well documented. See, e.g., Bulow et al. (2003).

[28] These wholesale prices are those paid by independently owned gas stations, either branded (e.g., Exxon or BP) or unbranded (not affiliated with a refiner). The wholesale price of gasoline paid by refiner owned stations is not publicly available.

[29] Fleet cards are often used by firms whose employees drive a lot for business purposes, e.g., salesman or insurance claims adjusters. Fleet cards are often used to closely monitor what items employees charge to the firm, e.g., to ensure that an employee only bills fuel and not food when visiting a filling station.

uses corresponds to a quantity weighted pricing scheme.[30] Second, branded gasoline stations (which tend to charge higher prices) are more likely to accept fleet cards. Thus, on any given day the average price reported by OPIS is likely higher than the (unobserved) average gasoline price in a market. For the purposes of this study, however, this should not be a problem because we are measuring changes in price levels across markets; that is, as long as the differential between branded and unbranded gasoline does not change as a result of the joint venture, this data should allow us to determine how the prices change following the joint venture.[31]

OPIS sells two types of retail price data (both types are used in this study). The first type of data consists of the daily prices by individual stations. OPIS also creates aggregate measures of prices for each of more than 360 metropolitan areas throughout the U.S. While OPIS reports daily price data, we have chosen to conduct our analysis using data aggregated to the weekly level. The composition of stations reporting price data on any day in the OPIS data changes from day to day. Thus, using daily data, it is not clear if prices in a market change from day to day because the composition of the sample changed (e.g., prices increased because a larger proportion of high priced stations report prices on a given day) or because the price distribution changed. By aggregating prices over a longer time period, changes in the composition of the sample are less of an issue.

For our two key regions, the Louisville and Chicago areas, we used OPIS's daily station-specific retail price data and OPIS's daily retailer-specific branded and unbranded wholesale prices. We constructed the average weekly retail price by taking the average of all station days reporting in a given week in the city of Louisville (Chicago). We focused on a region narrower than the metropolitan area for two reasons. First, all of our prices are measured before taxes. Taxes often vary by jurisdiction, e.g., taxes are different in the city of Chicago than elsewhere in Cook County, Illinois. By focusing on a specific jurisdiction, we can correctly measure a region's pre-tax price. Second, within the broad metropolitan area, different gasoline stations

---

[30]High frequency quantity data, e.g., daily or weekly, corresponding to gasoline station pricing data are not available.

[31]There is no discernable change in the branded/unbranded wholesale gasoline spread following the joint venture (results not shown, available on request from the authors).

may sell different specifications of gasoline (conventional or reformulated), or, alternatively, stations located on the periphery of the metropolitan area may sell RFG in competition with stations selling conventional gasoline. By focusing on stations in a specific city we can ensure that the sample stations face the same regulations and are selling the same type of gasoline. Wholesale (rack) prices are constructed by taking the average price of gasoline across all firms in a given week. Wholesale prices are calculated separately for branded and unbranded gasoline.

The retail and wholesale prices we use for the other control regions, Houston and Northern Virginia, are the aggregate prices sold by OPIS. We construct weekly retail prices by taking the average of the daily OPIS price in a given week. Similarly, the wholesale prices for Houston and Northern Virginia are constructed by taking the weekly average of the daily average branded and unbranded wholesale prices from OPIS.

Because most gasoline sold in the U.S., approximately 80 percent in 2002, is regular octane gasoline, we focus on the pricing of regular gasoline in this study. In checking the robustness of our empirical findings, however, we also examine the price of premium gasoline. Because a small proportion of gasoline sold is either premium or mid-grade, OPIS does not report station specific premium or mid-grade retail gasoline prices. OPIS does, however, construct aggregated daily premium retail gasoline prices. The premium retail gasoline prices analyzed in this study are all constructed by taking the weekly average of OPIS's reported daily prices.

Table 1 presents some descriptive statistics for wholesale and retail gasoline prices for all of the types of RFG examined in the study. The table shows that regular gasoline prices (net of taxes) and retail margins[32] (defined as the difference between retail price and wholesale price) are highest in Chicago. Wholesale regular prices and retail prices are the lowest in Houston, which is consistent with Houston being located in the region that exports gasoline to the rest of the U.S. Interestingly, retail margins on regular gasoline are quite similar in the city of Louisville and the

---

[32]Retail margins are calculated as the difference between the average retail price and the average branded rack price because the OPIS retail price measure systematically overrepresents branded gasoline stations. We do not report margins calculated relative to the unbranded rack price.

Houston and Northern Virginia metropolitan areas (and much lower than Chicago). The means of wholesale prices, retail prices and retail margins are different for premium gasoline. Wholesale prices of premium gasoline are more similar across the four cities than regular gasoline. The relative retail prices of regular and premium gasoline are significantly different for Chicago and Louisville, which is likely a result of sample composition (regular retail prices are the averages for stations in the cities of Chicago and Louisville, while premium prices are the OPIS reported average over the entire Chicago area and Kentucky portion of the Louisville metropolitan areas).

V. Empirical Analysis

We begin by presenting a simple graphical description of how wholesale and retail gasoline prices (and the implied retail margin) in Louisville changed following the MAP joint venture. Because gasoline prices are very volatile both over time and often between regions of the country, we need to explicitly control for how the relative price of gasoline changed in Louisville.[33] Figure III presents the difference in the wholesale price for branded gasoline,[34] the average retail price of gasoline,[35] and the retail margin (wholesale price-retail price) between Louisville and Chicago; that is, Figure III graphs the Louisville measure minus the Chicago measure (P_{Lt}-P_{Ct}). From Figure III we see that gasoline prices and retail margins were almost always higher in Chicago than Louisville. During the 1997-1999 time period, annual average wholesale prices, retail prices, and retail margins were about 1.2, 9.3, and 8.1 cents higher in Chicago than Louisville, respectively. In addition, the figure shows there were systematic seasonal differences in gasoline prices between Chicago and Louisville. Retail prices tended to

---

[33]For example the price of crude oil, the main input cost to making gasoline, went from near 10 dollars a barrel in 1998 to over 25 dollars a barrel in 1999.

[34]Because the gasoline stations sampled by OPIS are disproportionately branded, we use branded wholesale prices for our primary analysis. As discussed in more detail in this section, the same qualitative results are found using unbranded prices.

[35]Retail prices are calculated as the average over all stations in either the city of Louisville or the city of Chicago for a given week.

be relatively lower in Louisville at the end of the year, and wholesale prices tended to increase at the end of the year.

Following the MAP joint venture (January 1, 1998), there did not appear to be a systematic change in Louisville's retail prices relative to Chicago. Louisville's relative retail price appeared to have decreased in late 1998 and early 1999, but returned to 1997 levels by the end of 1999. In contrast, Louisville's wholesale price increased somewhat in 1998 (relative to 1997) and increased substantially roughly 15 months following the creation of MAP, and appeared to stay at this higher level for the remainder of the time period. These two findings suggest that the relative retail margin earned by gas stations in Louisville decreased substantially following the joint venture (the implied relative margin, (Retail Price$_L$ - Wholesale Price$_L$) - (Retail Price$_C$ - Wholesale Price$_C$) is plotted in Figure III).

To check the robustness of the pattern seen in Figure III, we plotted the wholesale and retail prices of gasoline in Louisville (and retail margins) relative to the three control regions: Chicago, Houston, and Northern Virginia.[36] Figure IV shows the difference between Louisville's branded wholesale gasoline prices and those of Chicago, Houston, and Northern Virginia in 1997, 1998, and 1999. While the average differential between Louisville and Houston, Northern Virginia, and Chicago were clearly different (Chicago has higher prices than Northern Virginia, which has higher prices than Houston), the changes in the differential overtime were very similar. The data clearly show that Louisville's relative wholesale price increased dramatically roughly 15 months after the merger. Figure V (for retail prices) and Figure VI (for retail margins) showed that the pattern for changes in retail prices and retail margins was quite similar when measured relative to Northern Virginia, Houston, or Chicago. Specifically, there did not appear to be any significant change in retail prices, but retail margins fell.

This pattern can be also be seen in the average annual differentials between Louisville and the control cities in Table 2. The mean difference between Louisville's rack price and Chicago's, Houston's , and Northern Virginia's rack priced increased by 5.4, 2.7, and 3.5 cents a gallon, respectively between 1997 and 1999. Similarly, between 1997 and 1999 relative retail

---

[36]Retail and wholesale prices for Northern Virginia and Houston are the OPIS calculated average prices.

margins in Louisville fell by about 5.7, 6.7, and 1.2 cents a gallon relative to Houston, Chicago, and Northern Virginia. In contrast, there is no systematic change in Louisville's relative gasoline prices following the merger.

Our next step is to determine if the empirical pattern seen in the plots (increased wholesale prices and decreased retail margins) is robust to controlling for seasonal effects. We do this using a simple difference-in-difference estimator. We assume that Louisville's retail prices, rack prices, and retail margins at a point in time are explained by expected crude oil prices (F_t),[37] changes induced by the joint venture (estimated separately for 1998 and 1999), seasonal effects (proxied by month dummies, D_{mt}), and time-specific supply and demand shocks (γ_t) as described by equation (1) below.

$$(1) \quad p_{Lt} = \alpha_0 + \alpha_1 F_t + \alpha_2 \text{If1998}_t + \alpha_3 \text{If1999}_t + \sum_{m=1}^{11} \beta_m D_{mt} + \gamma_t + \varepsilon_{Lt}$$

The prices (margins) in the control cities are explained by a similar relationship described by equation (2) below (the key difference being no systematic change induced by the joint venture).

$$(2) \quad p_{Ct} = \theta_0 + \theta_1 F_t + \sum_{m=1}^{11} \lambda_m D_{mt} + \gamma_t + \varepsilon_{Ct}$$

We allow for the possibility that the effect of future crude prices could have different effects on retail prices (margins) in different cities $(\alpha_1 \neq \theta_1)$, and that there may be systematic differences in seasonal pricing across regions $(\beta_m \neq \lambda_m)$.[38] Our key assumption required to identify the price changes caused by the joint venture is that the time-specific supply and demand shocks (γ_t) are common for Louisville and the control cities.

_____

[37]The crude oil futures price used is the New York Mercantile Exchange (NYMEX) contract for crude delivery at Cushing Oklahoma in the next month.

[38] There are persistent regional difference in seasonal changes in gasoline prices. For instance, different regions begin burning "summer" blends of gasoline at different times.

To estimate the price effects of the joint-venture we take the difference of equations (1) and (2) and estimate equation (3) below which eliminates the time-specific shocks to price (γ_t).

$$(3) \quad p_{Lt} - p_{Ct} = (\alpha_0 - \theta_0) + (\alpha_1 - \theta_1)F_t + \alpha_2 If1998_t + \alpha_3 If1999_t + \sum_{m=1}^{11} (\beta_m - \lambda_m)D_{mt} + (\varepsilon_{Lt} - \varepsilon_{Ct})$$

Because the error term of equation (3) is autoregressive, we estimate it using an ar(1) correction.[39] The parameter estimates of equation (3) for retail prices, rack prices, and retail margins are presented in Tables 3a, 3b, and 3c, respectively.

The general pattern of results seen in Figures IV, V, and VI is seen in the estimated price effects for 1998 and 1999. There is no consistent evidence showing a change in relative retail prices in Louisville. Louisville's retail price is essentially unchanged relative to Chicago, down two cents in 1999 relative to Houston, but up two cents relative to Northern Virginia. None of these price changes are statistically significant at conventional levels. In contrast, Louisville's rack prices may have increased slightly in 1998 (between 1.75 and 3.75 cents) and increased substantially in 1999 (between 3.25 and 6.75 cents).[40, 41] There is some difference across control cities in the change in relative retail margins. Relative to Chicago and Houston, retail margins in Louisville appear to have fallen about six cents in 1999. The relative decrease in Houston is much smaller, about 1.7 cents, and is not significant at conventional levels. In addition, a cursory view of the estimated coefficients on the month dummies shows that there are systematic differences in retail and rack prices overtime across cities; that is, the coefficients on the month dummies are both economically and statistically significantly different from zero.

---

[39]We use the Prais-Winsten correction for autocorrelation.

[40]The wholesale price increase in 1998 is not, however, robust to changes in the measure of the price of gasoline, see Table 3.

[41]The data appear to be stationary in the retail price and retail margin regressions. However, the error terms in the rack price regressions may be non-stationary. The autocorrelation coefficients are very large in these regressions: .98 for Chicago, .90 for Houston, and .86 for Virginia, and the null hypothesis of non-stationarity cannot be rejected for these regressions. Thus, the estimated standard errors must be viewed with caution. However, the pattern seen from these regressions is consistent with the figures and average differences shown in Table 2.

To test the robustness of our findings we examined the prices of two alternative types of RFG sold in Louisville and the control cities: unbranded gasoline and premium gasoline. Because the OPIS retail data oversamples branded gasoline, and because it is difficult to define exactly what an unbranded gasoline station is,[42] we conduct our primary analysis of wholesale gasoline pricing using branded gasoline. However, a priori, there may be reason to believe the price effects of the merger could differ for branded and unbranded gasolines sold in the wholesale market. In Louisville the creation of MAP did not affect the number of firms (six) typically posting wholesale prices for branded gasoline (Ashland did not sell branded gasoline in the wholesale market).[43] In contrast, for unbranded gasoline both Marathon and Ashland were important participants, and following the merger only three firms were typically selling unbranded RFG in Louisville.[44] Because branded wholesale gasoline typically sells at a premium of 1-2 cents a gallon relative to unbranded gasoline, following the creation of MAP the differential between branded and unbranded wholesale prices might converge.

There is also a differentiation between grades of gasoline based on the octane level of the gasoline. Most gasoline sold, 80 percent, is regular unleaded, with an octane rating between 85 and 88. Most of the remaining gasoline sold, 14 percent, is premium, with an octane rating of greater than 90.[45] Because there are different price cost margins on premium gasoline, see Barron et al. (2000), the creation of MAP could have different effects in this market segment.

The changes in relative prices appear to be essentially the same for premium gasoline (both branded and unbranded) and unbranded regular gasoline as for the base case of regular

---

[42]For example, in gasoline markets branded gasoline (sold through stations affiliated with major oil companies) typically sells at a premium relative to gasoline sold through unaffiliated stations (e.g., a local convenience stores). However, even within the branded gasolines there are real differences in pricing which make distinctions between branded and unbranded gasoline less meaningful. For example, in California, gasoline sold at ARCO stations often sells at a significant discount below the average price, but ARCO is clearly a "branded" station.

[43]The six firms were Amoco, BP, Chevron, Citgo, Marathon, Shell, and Sunoco.

[44]The three firms were MAP, BP, and S.R. & M.(Sunoco).

[45]A small amount of gasoline sold, six percent, is "mid-grade" with an octane rating between 88 and 90, which is a combination of regular and premium gasoline.

branded gasoline. Table 4 presents the estimated year effects from the regression of the Louisville measure on the control city measure, month dummies, and a futures price for oil which also corrects for autocorrelation; that is, the analogue to Tables 3a, 3b, and 3c. For brevity, we only report the coefficients and corresponding t-statistics for the year dummies. [46] The patterns for premium gasoline (both branded and unbranded) and unbranded regular gasoline are the same as in Tables 3a, 3b, and 3c. Rack prices for premium gasoline and unleaded gasoline increased by three to seven cents per gallon in 1999 relative to 1997 (depending on the control city).[47] Retail prices did not exhibit any systematic price change, and retail margins fell by two to seven cents per gallon, depending on the choice of control city.

VI. Interpreting the Results

The primary goal of this study is to determine if consumer prices increased as a result of the MAP joint venture. Our findings suggest that retail prices did not increase following the joint venture. This finding is robust to the choice of control city (Chicago, Louisville, or Northern Virginia) and grade of gasoline (regular/premium). We did, however, find a significant increase in wholesale (rack) prices which occurred roughly 15 months following the joint venture. This wholesale price increase is seen for both branded and unbranded gasoline and is robust to the grade of gasoline sold and choice of control city. While the wholesale price increase continues to the end of the sample period (through 1999), it is very difficult to determine if the differential disappears in 2000 or 2001.[48] (because of supply shocks affecting the Midwest region in 2000

---

[46]To facilitate comparison of the results, the estimates from Table 3a, 3b, and 3c are reproduced in Table 5.

[47]While the estimated year effect for wholesale gasoline in1998 (relative to 1997) is positive in all of the estimated specifications of equation 2, the year effect is not statistically significant for unbranded gasoline sold in Houston or Northern Virginia.

[48]The U.S. Midwest experienced multiple supply shocks in 2000 and 2001 that caused large movements in gasoline prices both within and between Midwestern cities. In particular, the differences between wholesale prices in Louisville and the control cities changed dramatically and frequently as gasoline markets responded to these supply shocks. For this reason, it is very

and 2001). The primary question is whether the change in wholesale pricing was related to the merger. A secondary question is why was there no overall change in retail pricing given the increase in wholesale prices. This section discusses there two issues.

The increase in relative rack prices in Louisville was not likely the result of the joint venture. Instead, rack prices appear to have increased because of a large increase in demand for the RFG in the Midwest that may not have been completely anticipated by refiners. This increase in demand was caused by St. Louis entering the RFG program.

Specifically, in the summer of 1999, the St. Louis MSA began using RFG. Prior to 1999, the St. Louis area used a low Reid vapor pressure conventional gasoline in an attempt to satisfy air quality requirements without using RFG. In 1998, after failing to meet federal clean air requirements and facing the possibility of losing federal highway funds, the Missouri legislature passed a bill removing the ban on RFG sales in the state and authorized the state to opt into the federal RFG program. The Missouri Governor then sent a letter to the EPA in the Summer of 1998 asking to opt into the RFG program. The EPA issued a proposed rule in September of 1998 and a final rule in February of 1999 which required refiners to supply RFG at wholesale by May 1, 1999 and retail by June 1, 1999. Industry articles suggest that the industry met the May 1 and June 1 deadlines. (Platt's Oilgram News, various issues)

There are a number of reasons to argue that St. Louis's switch to RFG was the source of the Louisville price spike. First, when St. Louis began using RFG, it was consuming essentially the same type of RFG as Louisville.[49] Second, both cities had the same source of marginal supply, gasoline imported from the Gulf area refineries either by barge or pipeline. Third, the increased demand for RFG resulting from St. Louis's entry into the federal reformulated program was substantial. While quantities of gasoline sold are not readily available at the MSA level, the state level data in this case is useful. The average monthly amount of RFG sold in Missouri

---

difficult to isolate any relatively small(three to five cent per gallon) permanent change in relative gasoline prices during this time period.

[49]Most of the gasoline consumed in St. Louis and Louisville was made with MTBE rather than ethanol. In contrast, all of the RFG consumed in Chicago was made with ethanol and produced locally by the Chicago area refiners.

(which is only consumed in St. Louis) for 1999 was 1.04 million gallons a day while the average amount of RFG sold in Kentucky (which is only sold in the Louisville area and Kentucky suburbs of Cincinnati) was 1.08 million gallons a day.[50] Thus, Midwest demand for RFG with MTBE essentially doubled in the spring/summer of 1999.[51]

The timing of Louisville's relative wholesale price increase for RFG is consistent with St. Louis entering the reformulated program. In order to meet the EPA requirement to have RFG available at wholesale by May 1, 1999, wholesalers in St. Louis would have to begin building inventories of RFG in late March or early April. This is when Louisville's relative RFG prices began to increase. Figure VII shows the difference in the rack prices between Louisville and Chicago for both conventional gasoline and RFG. Not only does this graph show the timing of the change in RFG pricing in April of 1999 but also shows that the relationship between Chicago and Louisville in conventional was unchanged during the three years as mentioned earlier.

In order to double the amount of RFG made with MTBE needed to supply the Midwest, refiners needed to change their output mix to less conventional gasoline (which had been consumed in St. Louis) to RFG. Recent studies, see Bulow et al (2003) and Taylor and Fischer (2003), suggest that modifying refineries to produce new specifications of gasoline is complicated and can lead to unexpected output reductions. For example, a change in the RFG specifications in 2000 substantially reduced local refining capacity in the upper Midwest that increased the price of gasoline in the Chicago/Milwaukee area.

An additional fact consistent with there being a supply shock in Louisville is the change in the difference between the rack and the DTW prices in 1999. In other markets experiencing supply disruptions (the Midwest in 2000, California in 1999 and 2000), stations supplied directly by refiners (DTW stations) experience less of a wholesale price increase than those stations that

---

[50]Department of Energy, Energy Information Administration, Petroleum Marketing Annual, 1998 and 1998.

[51]In addition, the average amount of RFG sold in Louisville in 1999, 1.08 million gallons a day, was over 14 percent higher than in 1998, 947.5 thousand gallons a day. While it is not clear what caused the increased demand in Louisville, it is hard to argue that there was an anticompetitive effect from this merger with an increase in sales of 14 percent.

purchase their gasoline in at the rack.[52] Normally the rack price is less than the DTW price because the rack price does not include delivery or additional services.

The pricing pattern in Louisville in mid to late 1999 is similar to that observed in other regions experiencing supply disruptions. A comparison of the rack and DTW prices for RFG gasoline in Kentucky shows that there was a change in relative prices in 1999. The difference between the DTW price and the rack price in Kentucky, shown in Figure VIII, averaged 4-5 cents per gallon in 1997 and 1998. In 1999 the difference between DTW and rack prices was historically low and was *negative* for a few months. This drop in the DTW-to-rack spread coincides with the increase in rack prices which began in April 1999.

The change in relative prices between the rack and the DTW prices for reformulated gasoline at wholesale also suggests an explanation for the lack of pass through between wholesale and retail prices. The rack price represents the wholesale price for a portion of the stations in a market that are supplied from the rack. The remainder of the stations are either lessee dealers which pay the DTW price or the company owned and operated stations which pay an internal transfer price. Our findings shows that the rack supplied stations experienced a relative wholesale price increase for RFG of 3-5 cents per gallon. In contrast, the differential between rack and DTW prices decreased by 3-5 cents per gallon (DTW became relatively less expensive). These two facts imply that DTW stations experienced virtually *no change* in relative wholesale price. DTW stations make up a significant proportion of the stations in Louisville. According to the New Image Marketing survey(s) of the gasoline stations in Louisville, 22 percent of the stations are direct supplied (either DTW or company operated) by a count of the number of stations. When weighted by the estimated number of gallons sold the direct supplied stations represent 30 percent of the stations in Louisville. Thus, rack supplied stations were competing with DTW and company owned stations (accounting for 30% of sales) that did not experience an increase in relative wholesale prices. This certainly inhibited the ability of rack-supplied stations to pass through their increased wholesale prices. Estimating a model of the average weekly price of gasoline by station on ownership type, described in the appendix, shows

---

[52]Department of Energy, Energy Information Administration, Petroleum Marketing Annual, 1999 and 2000.

that the price of gasoline at rack supplied stations increased from 1998 to 1999 relative to the direct supplied stations by about 0.5 cents per gallon.

Additionally, as shown in Figure II, the reformulated area in Louisville is not particularly large, a little over 20 by 20 miles, and is surrounded on all sides by stations selling conventional gasoline. Thus stations paying the rack price for gasoline are competing with direct served stations, which also did not experience the relative wholesale price increase, and are also competing with stations across the Indiana border and further out in Kentucky that sell conventional gasoline, which did not experience a relative price increase. Apparently these factors kept stations supplied by the rack in Louisville from passing through enough of the price increase to affect average retail prices.

VII. Conclusions

This study uses retail gasoline prices and wholesale (rack) gasoline prices for Louisville and a number of control cities to examine the price effects of the Marathon-Ashland joint venture. We find no effect of this transaction on the retail price of RFG or conventional gasoline in Louisville. Wholesale (rack) RFG prices increased significantly 15 months after the transaction. This increase coincided with a major industry event which affected the Midwestern gasoline area, the introduction of RFG in St. Louis. The available evidence suggests that St. Louis's decision to switch to RFG may have resulted in the increase in Louisville's rack price for RFG. In particular, the demand in the Midwest for RFG made with MTBE (the RFG used in St. Louis and Louisville but not Chicago) nearly doubled with St. Louis's entry into the RFG program. Further, the inversion in rack and DTW wholesale prices for RFG is consistent what has been observed in other markets that have experienced supply shocks.

The results of the this study reveal the importance of examining both retail and wholesale pricing in measuring the competitive effects of mergers. Had we analyzed rack prices without examining retail pricing, we would have concluded that the transaction led to higher prices. Further, the observation that the rack price increased and did not seem to be passed through by retailers caused us to do additional research into what shocks would have affected rack but not retail prices.[53] Our results suggest that researchers should be very careful in using rack prices as a measure of the wholesale price of gasoline, particularly in markets experiencing supply shocks, e.g., the Midwest or California. The wholesale price that different types of gasoline retailers (e.g., DTW or rack-supplied) pay may vary significantly during a supply shock.

The results of this study suggest that this merger in a moderately/highly concentrated market did not raise consumer prices. Given the large changes in market structure in petroleum markets, additional research into the competitive effects of mergers would be beneficial. Because of the idosyncratic nature of oil markets, e.g. different sources of marginal supply, different fuel specifications, etc., the results of any one study need to be qualified. Only when a sufficient number of merger retrospectives are complete will it be possible to generalize the results to inform antitrust policy.

---

[53]To our knowledge, no article in the trade press noted a relative increase in Louisville's rack price, and no article described how St. Louis's entry into the RFG program might affect gasoline pricing in the Midwest.

Bibliography

Barron J. and J. Umbeck, "The Effects of Different Contractual Arrangements: The Case of Retail Gasoline Markets," *Journal of Law and Economics*, 27(2), October 1984, pp. 313-328.

Barron, J., B. Taylor, and J. Umbeck, "A Theory of Quality-Related Differences in Retail Margins: Why There is a "Premium on Premium Gasoline," *Economic Inquiry*, 38(4), October 2000, pp. 550-569.

Barton, D.M., and R. Sherman,"The Price and Profit Effects of Horizontal Merger: A Case Study", *Journal of Industrial Economics*, 33(2), December 1984, pp. 165-77.

Blass A., and D. Carlton, "The Choice of Organizational Form in Gasoline Retailing and the Cost of Laws That Limit That Choice," *Journal of Law and Economics*, 44(2), Oct. 2001, pp. 511-24.

Borenstein, S. and Shepard, A., "Dynamic Pricing in Retail Gasoline Markets," *The RAND Journal of Economics*, 27(3), Autumn 1996, pp. 429-451.

Bulow, J. , J. Fischer, J. Creswell, C. Taylor, "U.S. Midwest Gasoline Pricing and the Spring 2000 Price Spike," *Energy Journal*, 24(3), 2003, pp. 121-49

Chouinard H. And J. Perloff, "Gasoline Price Differences: Taxes, Pollution Regulations, Mergers, Market Power, and Market Conditions," August 2001.

Evans, W., L. Froeb, and G. Werden, "Endogeneity in the Concentration–Price Relationship: Causes, Consequences, and Cures," *Journal of Industrial Economics,* 41, 1993, pp. 431-438

Froeb, L., S. Tschantz, and G. Werden, "Vertical Restraints and the Effects of Upstream Horizontal Mergers," Owen Graduate School of Management Working Paper, March 27, 2002.

Focarelli D. and F. Panetta, "Are Mergers Beneficial to Consumers? Evidence from the Market for Bank Deposits," *American Economic Review*, 93(4), September 2003, pp. 1152-1172.

Hastings, J. "Vertical Relationships and Competition in Retail Gasoline Markets: Empirical Evidence from Contract Changes in Southern California," *American Economic Review*, 94(1), March 2004, pp. 317-328.

Hastings J. and R. Gilbert, "Market Power, Vertical Integration and the Wholesale Price of Gasoline," 2002, working paper.

Kim,E.H, and V. Singal,"Mergers and Market Power: Evidence from the Airline Industry," *American Economic Review*, 83(3), June 1993, pp. 549-69.

Manusazak, M, "The Impact of Upstream Mergers on Retail Gasoline Markets," September 2002, working paper.

Pautler, P., "Evidence on Mergers and Acquisitions," *Antitrust Bulletin*, 48(1), Spring 2003, pp. 119-221.

Ordover, J, G. Saloner, S. Salop, "Equilibrium Vertical Foreclosure," *American Economic Review*, 80(1), March 1990, pp. 127-142.

Schumann, L., J. Reitzes, and R. Rogers, "In the Matter of Weyerhaeuser Company: The Use of a Hold-Separate Order in a Merger with Horizontal and Vertical Effects," *Journal of Regulatory Economics*, 11(3), May 1997, pp. 271-89.

Schumann, L., R. Rogers, and J. Reitzes, *Case Studies of The Price Effects of Horizontal Mergers*, Federal Trade Commission, April 1992.

Shepard, A., "Contractual Form, Retail Price and Asset Characteristics," *Rand Journal of Economics*, 24, Spring 1993 pp. 58-77

Taylor, C. and J. Fischer, "A Review of West Coast Gasoline Pricing and the Impact of Regulations," *International Journal of the Economics of Business*, 10(2), July 2003, pp. 225-243.

U. S. Government Accounting Office, "Energy Prices: Gasoline Price Increases in Early 1985 Interrupted Previous Trend," September 1986.

Vita, M. and S. Sacher, "The Competitive Effects of Not-for-Profit Hospital Mergers: A Case Study," *Journal of Industrial Economics,* 49(1), March 2001, pp. 63-84.

Vita, M., "Regulatory Restrictions on Vertical Integration and Control: The Competitive Impact of Gasoline Divorcement Policies," *Journal of Regulatory Economics*, 18(3), November 2000, pp. 217-33.

Appendix - The Impact on Retail Prices of a Rack Price Increase

In this section of the paper we provide some explanation for why the relative rack price increase Louisville experienced in mid-to-late 1999 did not manifest itself in a significant increase in retail price. As described in the industry background section, different gas stations face different wholesale prices depending on their source of supply. In particular, aggregate gasoline pricing data from EIA suggests that during the period in which Louisville experienced a relative increase in rack prices direct supplied stations *did not* experience a price increase (see Figure VIII). Thus, rack supplied stations were forced to compete with direct supplied stations that did not have the relative wholesale price increase. Further, direct supplied stations make up a significant fraction of gasoline stations in Louisville, roughly one third. If the direct supplied stations were located close to rack supplied stations and sold similar qualities of gasoline (brands consumers view as similar), then rack supplied stations may have found it difficult to pass much of their relative price increase through to consumers. However, because there is some differentiation among gas stations (either from location or brand) there would like be some change in the relative retail prices. We will examine if, on average, rack-supplied stations retail prices increased relative to direct supplied stations retail prices during the wholesale price spike, 1999.

In order to measure the effect of being rack supplied or direct supplied on retail price it is important to control for station specific characteristics such as locational rents. For example, if more densely populated areas are more likely to have more company operated stations and these are directly supplied then on average directly supplied stations will have higher prices. For this reason we include station-specific fixed effects in our analysis of gas stations retail prices.

In our empirical analysis we use data from the New Image Marketing gasoline station surveys, 1996, 1997 and 1999, to determine which gasoline stations were supplied via the rack or were directly supplied by refiners. We test to determine if the relative price of gasoline at stations supplied from the rack increased relative to direct supplied stations using a two part estimation procedure. First we estimate a retail price as a function of the rack price (the wholesale price to roughly two-thirds of gasoline stations), week dummies (to control for seasonality) and station specific fixed effects (see equation 1 below). Second, we examine the average residuals in 1998 and 1999 separately for direct and rack supplied stations to determine if relative prices changed for direct supplied and rack supplied stations.

$$(1)\ \text{Retail Price}_{it} = B_1 \text{Rack Price}_{it} + B_2 \text{Week1}_{it} + ... + B_n \text{Week51}_{it} + \alpha_i + \varepsilon_{it}$$

The retail prices used in the regression were the price charged by a given station on a given day (all observed days are weekdays). The rack price was the average branded rack price observed on that day in Louisville. There were 368 gasoline stations in the sample, 81 were rack supplied.

The explanatory variables in equation 1 explain 82 percent of the variation in the retail prices. Figure A-1 shows the average residuals for the direct supplied and the rack supplied stations. The figure shows that the residuals of rack supplied stations increased relative to direct supplied stations during the relative spike in Louisville rack prices.

A comparison of the mean residuals by source of station supply (see Table A1 below), shows that the relative price of rack-supplied stations increased by approximately 0.6 cents per gallon in 1999 relative to 1998.

Table A1 - Average Residuals by Year and Supply Type

	Year -1998	Year - 1999
Rack	-0.32	0.38
	(0.02)	(0.02)
Direct	-0.09	0.04
	(0.01)	(0.01)
Difference	-0.23*	0.34*
	(0.02)	(0.02)

Table 1: Descriptive Statistics For Gasoline Prices and Margins
(Prices exclude all taxes)

Variable Name	City	Branded/Unbranded	Weeks	Mean	Standard Deviation	Min	Max
Premium Retail Margin	Chicago	Branded	155	16.39	3.93	5.25	27.37
Premium Retail Margin	Houston	Branded	155	17.23	3.31	8.85	24.73
Premium Retail Margin	Louisville	Branded	155	18.41	4.56	7.13	28.19
Premium Retail Margin	Virginia	Branded	155	15.12	4.41	3.82	23.80
Regular Retail Margin	Chicago	Branded	154	22.92	4.01	12.25	33.47
Regular Retail Margin	Houston	Branded	155	13.19	3.30	6.50	21.81
Regular Retail Margin	Louisville	Branded	154	14.84	4.07	3.54	23.97
Regular Retail Margin	Virginia	Branded	155	13.08	4.03	4.09	20.40
Retail Price Premium Gas	Chicago	n/a	155	89.65	10.46	65.66	105.95
Retail Price Premium Gas	Houston	n/a	155	82.98	10.18	63.49	101.21
Retail Price Premium Gas	Louisville	n/a	155	89.93	13.11	59.73	113.84
Retail Price Premium Gas	Virginia	n/a	155	85.23	11.77	61.61	102.49
Retail Price Regular Gas	Chicago	n/a	154	86.18	8.97	66.25	99.75
Retail Price Regular Gas	Houston	n/a	155	69.07	9.29	51.28	85.70
Retail Price Regular Gas	Louisville	n/a	154	76.85	11.63	49.17	97.17
Retail Price Regular Gas	Virginia	n/a	155	72.24	10.59	50.98	87.78
Rack Price Premium Gas	Chicago	Branded	156	73.35	9.91	50.17	90.11
Rack Price Premium Gas	Houston	Branded	156	65.86	10.30	44.50	84.40
Rack Price Premium Gas	Louisville	Branded	156	71.66	12.15	44.96	94.44
Rack Price Premium Gas	Virginia	Branded	156	70.23	10.74	48.83	88.49
Rack Price Premium Gas	Chicago	Unbranded	156	70.51	10.11	46.28	89.02
Rack Price Premium Gas	Houston	Unbranded	156	63.75	11.10	39.84	81.53
Rack Price Premium Gas	Louisville	Unbranded	156	70.03	12.25	41.73	93.83
Rack Price Premium Gas	Virginia	Unbranded	156	64.32	11.53	39.15	82.50
Rack Price Regular Gas	Chicago	Branded	156	63.46	10.21	39.69	81.38
Rack Price Regular Gas	Houston	Branded	156	56.00	10.32	34.55	74.47
Rack Price Regular Gas	Louisville	Branded	156	62.29	12.19	35.40	84.96
Rack Price Regular Gas	Virginia	Branded	156	59.28	10.77	37.83	77.64
Rack Price Regular Gas	Chicago	Unbranded	156	61.85	10.17	38.15	80.35
Rack Price Regular Gas	Houston	Unbranded	156	55.09	10.96	31.36	73.40
Rack Price Regular Gas	Louisville	Unbranded	156	61.58	12.42	33.23	85.57
Rack Price Regular Gas	Virginia	Unbranded	156	57.77	11.08	33.83	76.81

Table 2: Mean Differential Between Louisville and Control City By Year
(Louisville Measure-Control City Measure)

Measure	Control City	1997	1998	1999
Margin	Houston	4.28	1.95	-1.44
Margin	Chicago	-5.24	-7.24	-11.91
Margin	Northern Virginia	2.15	2.03	0.97
Rack	Houston	5.78	4.60	8.49
Rack	Chicago	-2.63	-3.67	2.78
Rack	Northern Virginia	1.93	1.71	5.40
Retail	Houston	10.07	6.56	6.95
Retail	Chicago	-7.87	-10.91	-9.21
Retail	Northern Virginia	4.08	3.74	6.29

Table 3a: Regression of Difference in Louisville and Control City
Retail Price on Futures Price and Month Indicators

	Chicago Coefficient	Chicago Standard Error	Houston Coefficient	Houston Standard Error	Virginia Coefficient	Virginia Standard Error
1998 Indicator	0.73	1.40	-1.07	1.48	0.99	1.65
1999 Indicator	0.10	1.47	-2.51	1.51	2.23	1.88
January	-0.66	1.24	0.66	1.33	-1.63	1.43
February	1.42	1.45	2.20	1.55	0.24	1.65
March	2.14	1.53	3.27	1.63	1.28	1.75
April	3.36	1.58	3.96	1.68	1.87	1.82
May	2.66	1.61	4.58	1.72	3.23	1.86
June	3.27	1.62	5.71	1.73	4.51	1.87
July	1.45	1.58	4.07	1.68	3.39	1.82
August	0.83	1.55	2.88	1.66	2.70	1.78
September	-0.69	1.47	0.91	1.58	0.99	1.66
October	-0.45	1.32	0.09	1.42	-0.06	1.48
November	0.13	1.04	0.46	1.13	0.31	1.14
Futures Price	0.64	0.15	0.46	0.16	0.28	0.18
Constant	-22.28	3.49	-1.64	3.69	-2.73	4.12
rho	0.78		0.77		0.82	

Prais-Winsten Autocorrelation Correction

Table 3b: Regression of Difference in Louisville and Control City Rack Price on Futures Price and Month Indicators

	Chicago Coefficient	Chicago Standard Error	Houston Coefficient	Houston Standard Error	Virginia Coefficient	Virginia Standard Error
1998 Indicator	3.76	1.37	1.73	0.89	1.86	0.81
1999 Indicator	6.77	2.50	3.26	1.30	4.08	1.05
January	-3.32	1.19	-1.88	0.75	-2.38	0.69
February	-3.24	1.16	-2.10	0.82	-2.31	0.78
March	-2.76	1.13	-1.94	0.86	-1.84	0.82
April	-1.72	1.09	-0.49	0.89	-0.34	0.86
May	-1.88	1.04	0.02	0.90	0.04	0.87
June	-1.46	0.99	-0.13	0.89	0.08	0.87
July	-0.98	0.92	0.04	0.86	0.10	0.85
August	-0.59	0.84	-0.14	0.82	-0.25	0.82
September	-0.51	0.73	0.17	0.75	0.11	0.75
October	-0.38	0.61	-0.34	0.65	-0.51	0.66
November	-0.58	0.44	-0.09	0.49	-0.14	0.50
Futures Price	-0.06	0.09	0.37	0.09	0.31	0.09
Constant	-1.40	3.14	-1.62	2.06	-4.13	1.94
rho	0.98		0.90		0.86	

Prais-Winsten Autocorrelation Correction

Table 3c: Regression of Difference in Louisville and Control City Retail Margin on Futures Price and Month Indicators

	Chicago Coefficient	Chicago Standard Error	Houston Coefficient	Houston Standard Error	Virginia Coefficient	Virginia Standard Error
1998 Indicator	-1.61	1.37	-2.33	1.34	-0.73	1.48
1999 Indicator	-6.27	1.33	-5.81	1.22	-1.69	1.45
January	3.11	1.26	2.88	1.30	0.92	1.37
February	5.08	1.46	4.55	1.50	2.71	1.59
March	5.49	1.54	5.23	1.56	3.34	1.67
April	5.38	1.57	3.86	1.57	2.38	1.70
May	4.83	1.60	3.55	1.61	3.36	1.74
June	4.78	1.61	4.73	1.61	4.51	1.75
July	2.32	1.57	2.99	1.57	3.22	1.70
August	0.79	1.56	1.84	1.57	2.59	1.69
September	-0.80	1.49	-0.23	1.52	0.51	1.62
October	-0.81	1.36	-0.31	1.40	0.14	1.47
November	0.20	1.09	-0.01	1.16	0.16	1.18
Futures Price	0.28	0.15	0.08	0.15	-0.04	0.16
Constant	-13.08	3.40	0.41	3.34	1.29	3.70
rho	0.74		0.69		0.74	

Prais-Winsten Autocorrelation Correction

Table 4: Year Effects from Regression of Difference in Louisville and Control City Measure on Month Dummies, and Crude Oil Futures Price for Branded, Unbranded, Regular and Premium Gasoline

Measure	Type of Gasoline	Control City	Branded/Unbranded	Dummy:1998	T-Stat	Dummy: 1999	T-Stat
Margin	Premium Gas	Chicago	Branded	-1.63	-1.10	-5.35	-3.61
Margin	unleaded gas	Chicago	Branded	-1.61	-1.18	-6.27	-4.70
Margin	Premium Gas	Chicago	Unbranded	-2.13	-1.36	-7.38	-4.80
Margin	unleaded gas	Chicago	Unbranded	-1.59	-1.28	-6.69	-6.01
Margin	Premium Gas	Houston	Branded	-2.11	-1.37	-6.03	-4.87
Margin	unleaded gas	Houston	Branded	-2.32	-1.74	-5.81	-4.75
Margin	Premium Gas	Houston	Unbranded	-3.26	-2.33	-7.90	-6.35
Margin	unleaded gas	Houston	Unbranded	-3.23	-2.26	-7.49	-5.70
Margin	Premium Gas	Virginia	Branded	-0.30	-0.19	-1.46	-0.99
Margin	unleaded gas	Virginia	Branded	-0.73	-0.49	-1.69	-1.16
Margin	Premium Gas	Virginia	Unbranded	-0.87	-0.56	-2.50	-1.74
Margin	unleaded gas	Virginia	Unbranded	-0.91	-0.60	-2.35	-1.60
Rack	Premium Gas	Chicago	Branded	3.42	2.40	6.15	2.36
Rack	unleaded gas	Chicago	Branded	3.76	2.75	6.77	2.71
Rack	Premium Gas	Chicago	Unbranded	3.60	2.07	7.63	3.09
Rack	unleaded gas	Chicago	Unbranded	3.27	2.17	6.91	2.61
Rack	Premium Gas	Houston	Branded	1.71	1.91	3.29	2.53
Rack	unleaded gas	Houston	Branded	1.73	1.95	3.26	2.52
Rack	Premium Gas	Houston	Unbranded	1.75	1.84	4.93	4.37
Rack	unleaded gas	Houston	Unbranded	1.53	1.46	4.38	3.03
Rack	Premium Gas	Virginia	Branded	1.94	2.42	4.35	4.22
Rack	unleaded gas	Virginia	Branded	1.86	2.31	4.08	3.89
Rack	Premium Gas	Virginia	Unbranded	1.92	1.73	5.09	3.41
Rack	unleaded gas	Virginia	Unbranded	1.56	1.45	4.38	2.85
Retail	Premium Gas	Chicago	Branded	-0.05	-0.03	-0.04	-0.02
Retail	unleaded gas	Chicago	Branded	0.73	0.52	0.10	0.07
Retail	Premium Gas	Houston	Branded	-0.99	-0.67	-2.75	-1.87
Retail	unleaded gas	Houston	Branded	-1.06	-0.72	-2.51	-1.66
Retail	Premium Gas	Virginia	Branded	1.34	0.80	2.65	1.47
Retail	unleaded gas	Virginia	Branded	0.99	0.60	2.23	1.19

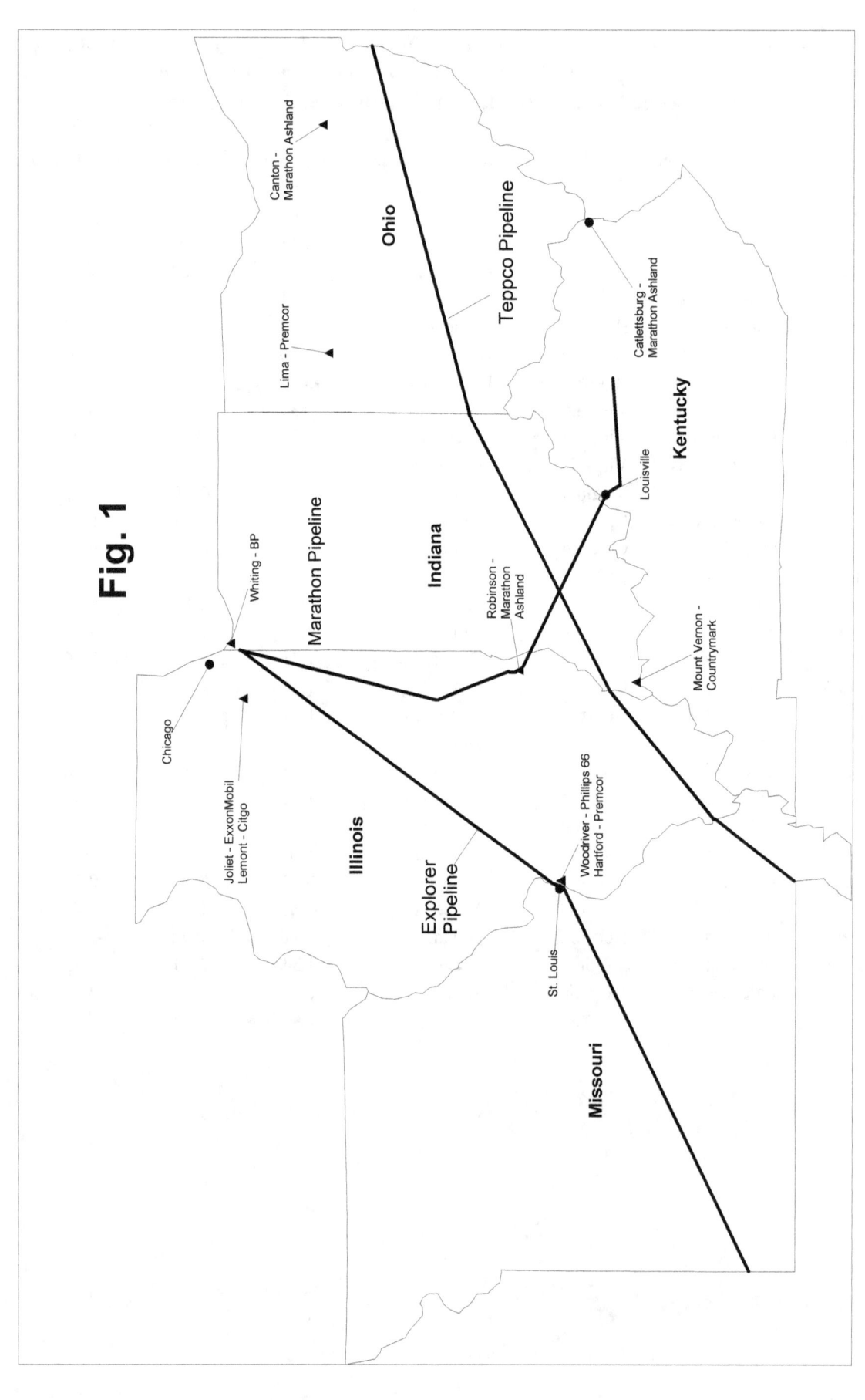

Fig. 1

Figure II

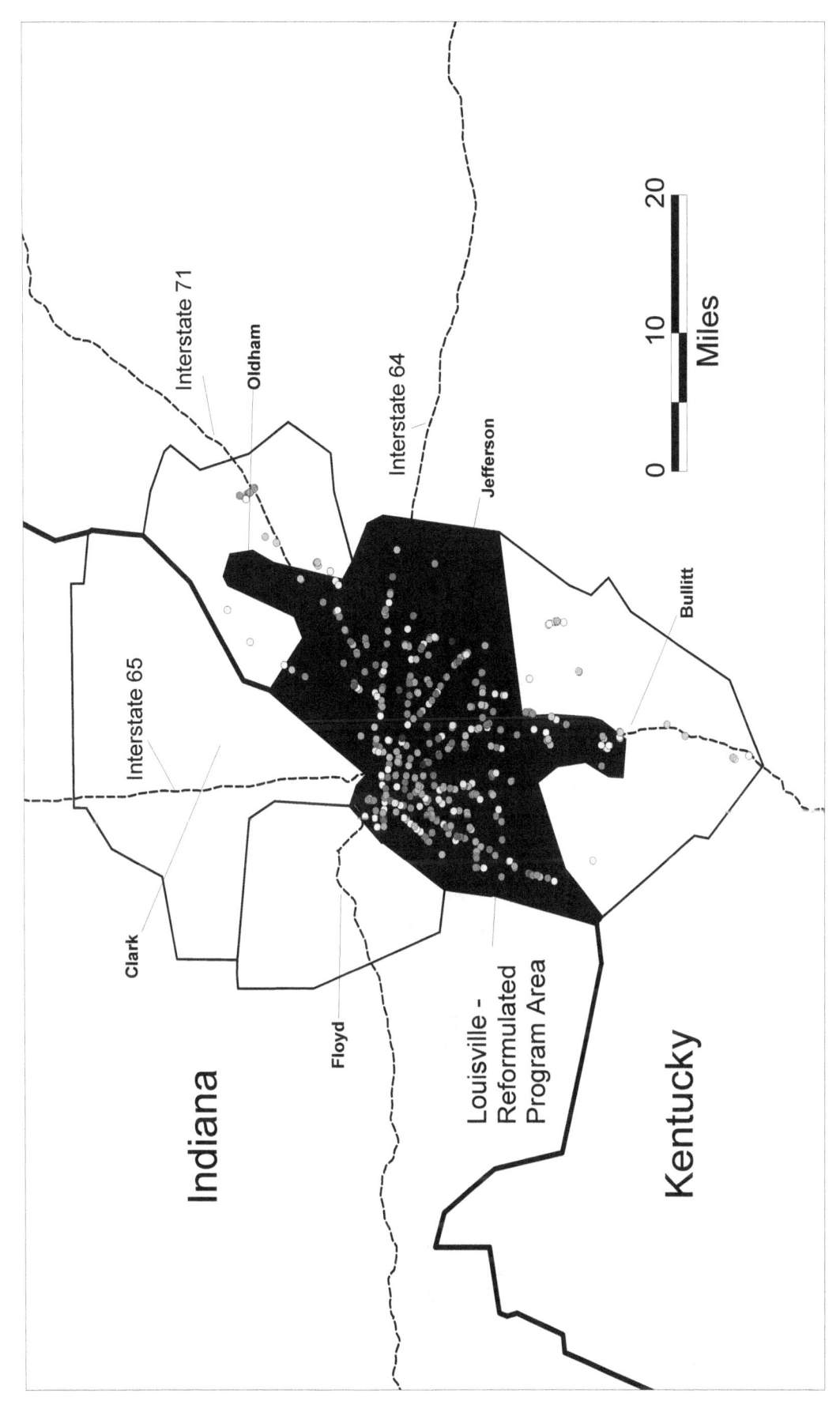

Indiana

Clark

Floyd

Interstate 65

Interstate 71

Oldham

Interstate 64

Jefferson

Louisville -
Reformulated
Program Area

Bullitt

Kentucky

0   10   20

Miles

Figure III
Difference in Louisville and Chicago Branded Rack Price, Retail Price, and Retail Margin

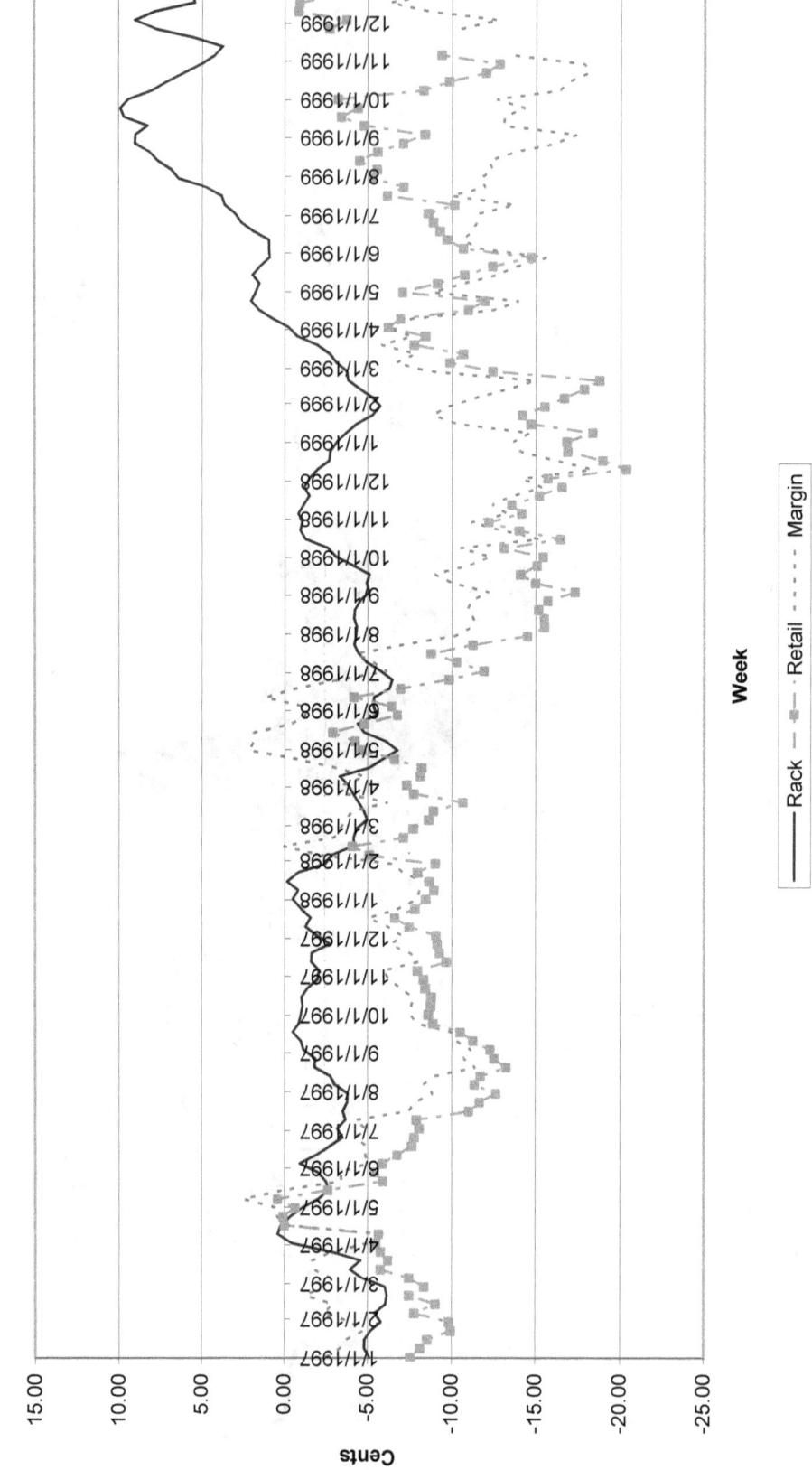

Week

——— Rack — ■ — Retail - - - - Margin

Figure IV
Difference in Branded Rack Prices Between Louisville and Control Cities

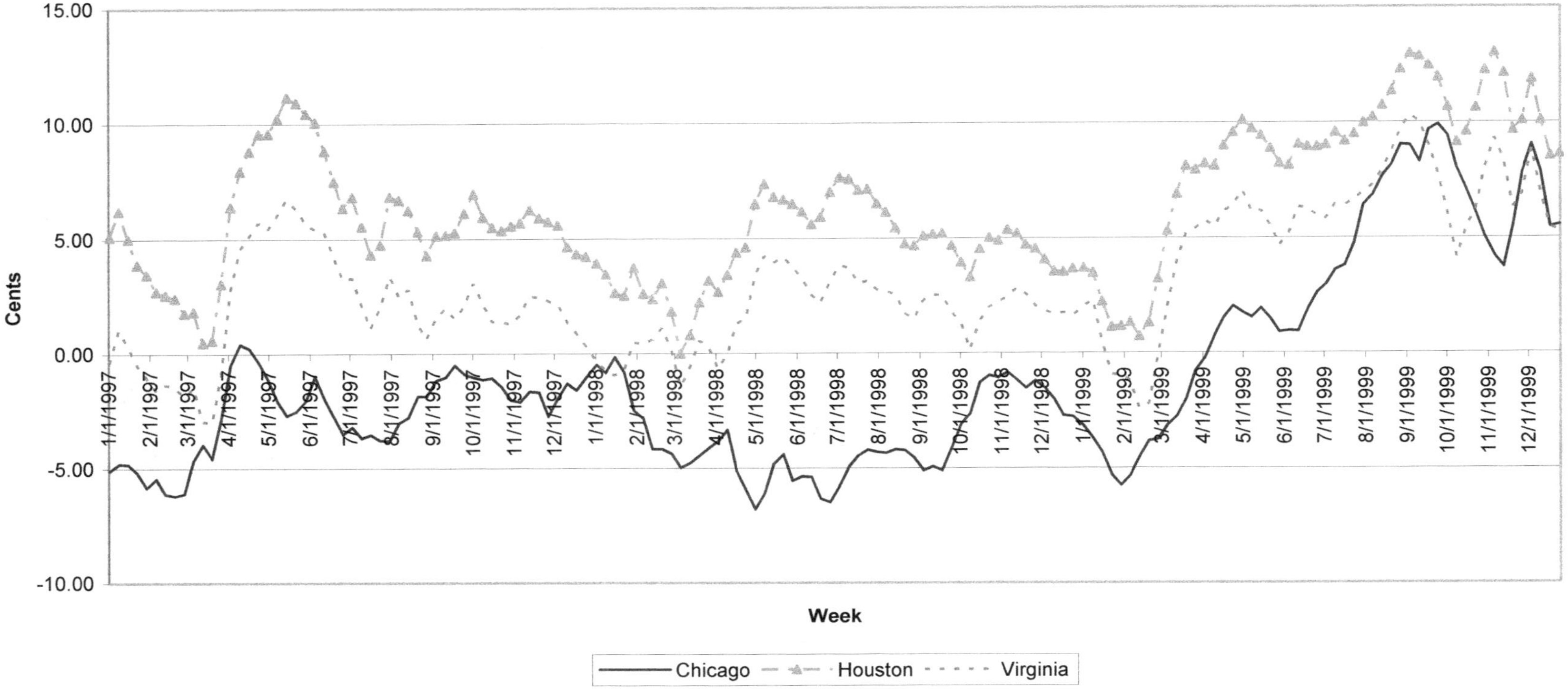

Week

Chicago — — — Houston - - - - - Virginia

Figure V
Difference Between Louisville Retail Price and Control Cities

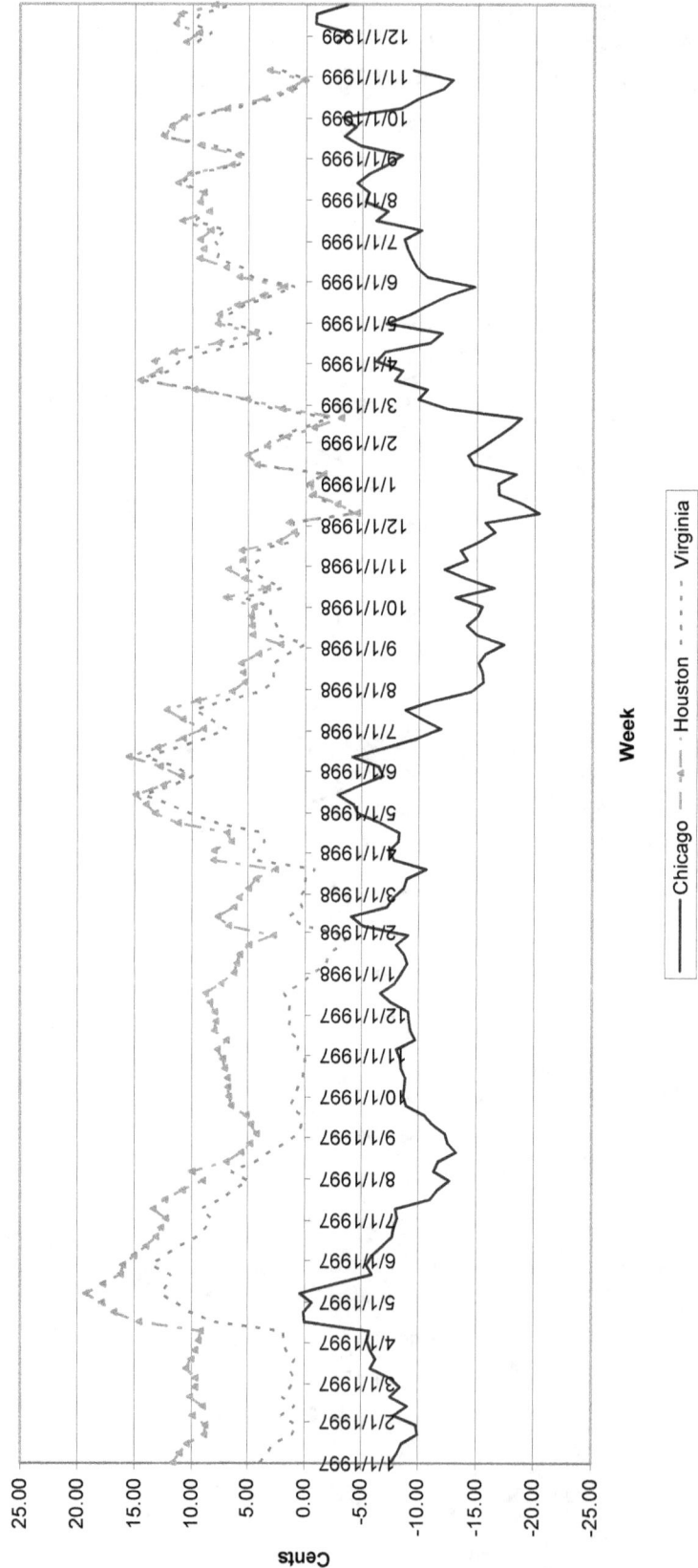

Week

Cents

—— Chicago — ▲ — Houston - - - - - Virginia

Figure VI
Difference Between Louisville and Control Cities Retail Margin

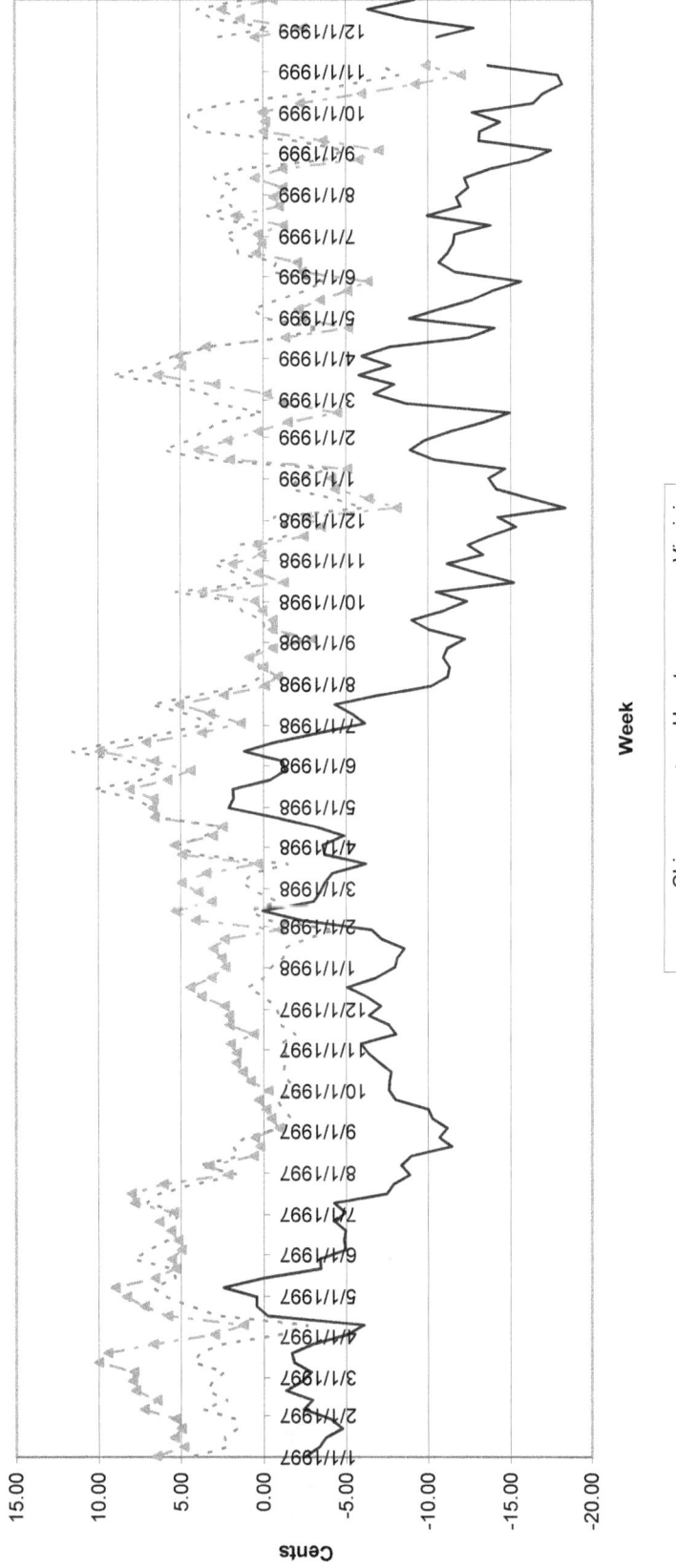

Figure VII
Difference Between Louisville and Chicago Unbranded Rack Prices for Conventional and Reformulated Gasoline

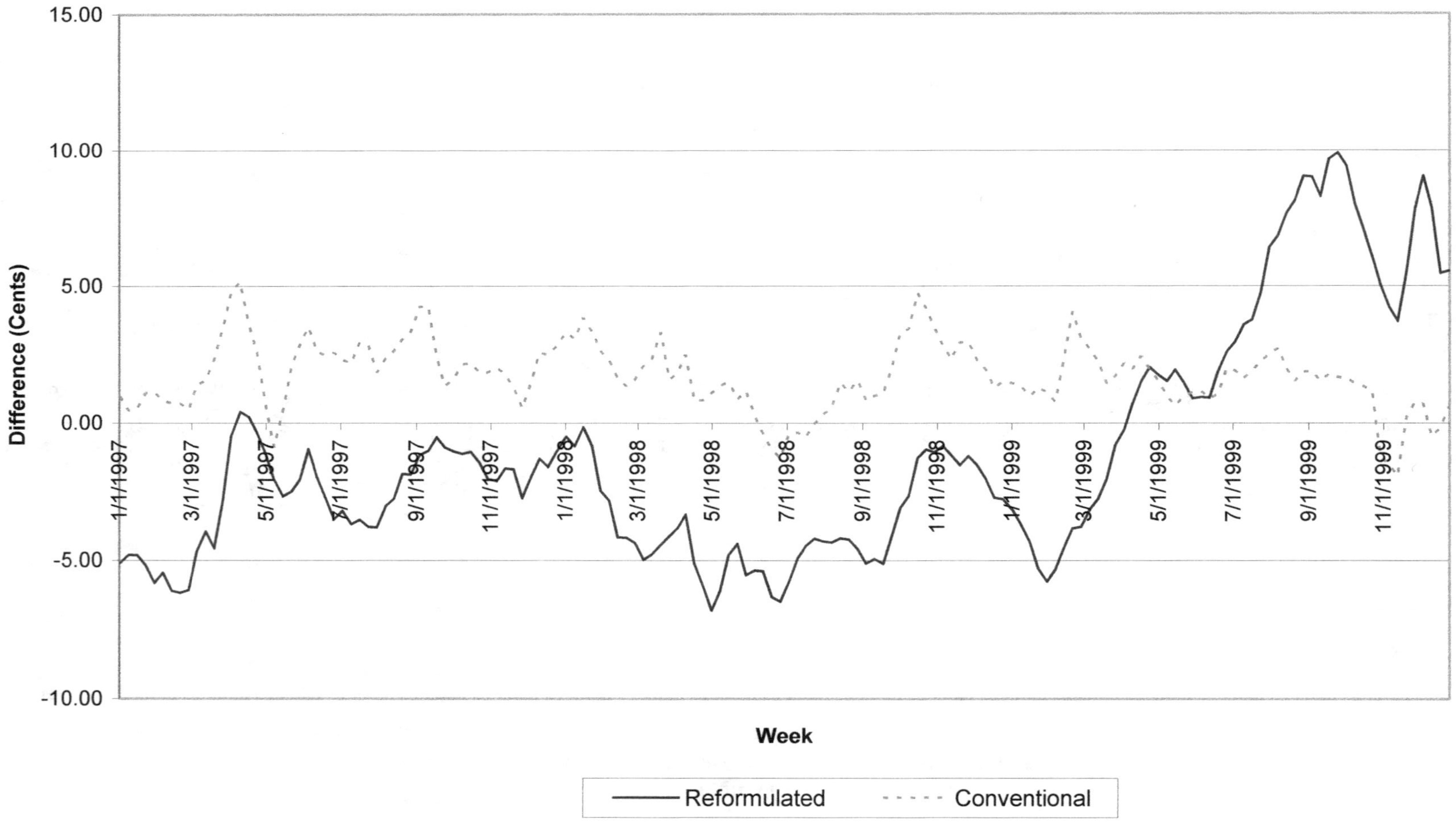

Figure VIII
Difference Between Kentucky Dealer Tank Wagon and Rack Prices(1997-1999)

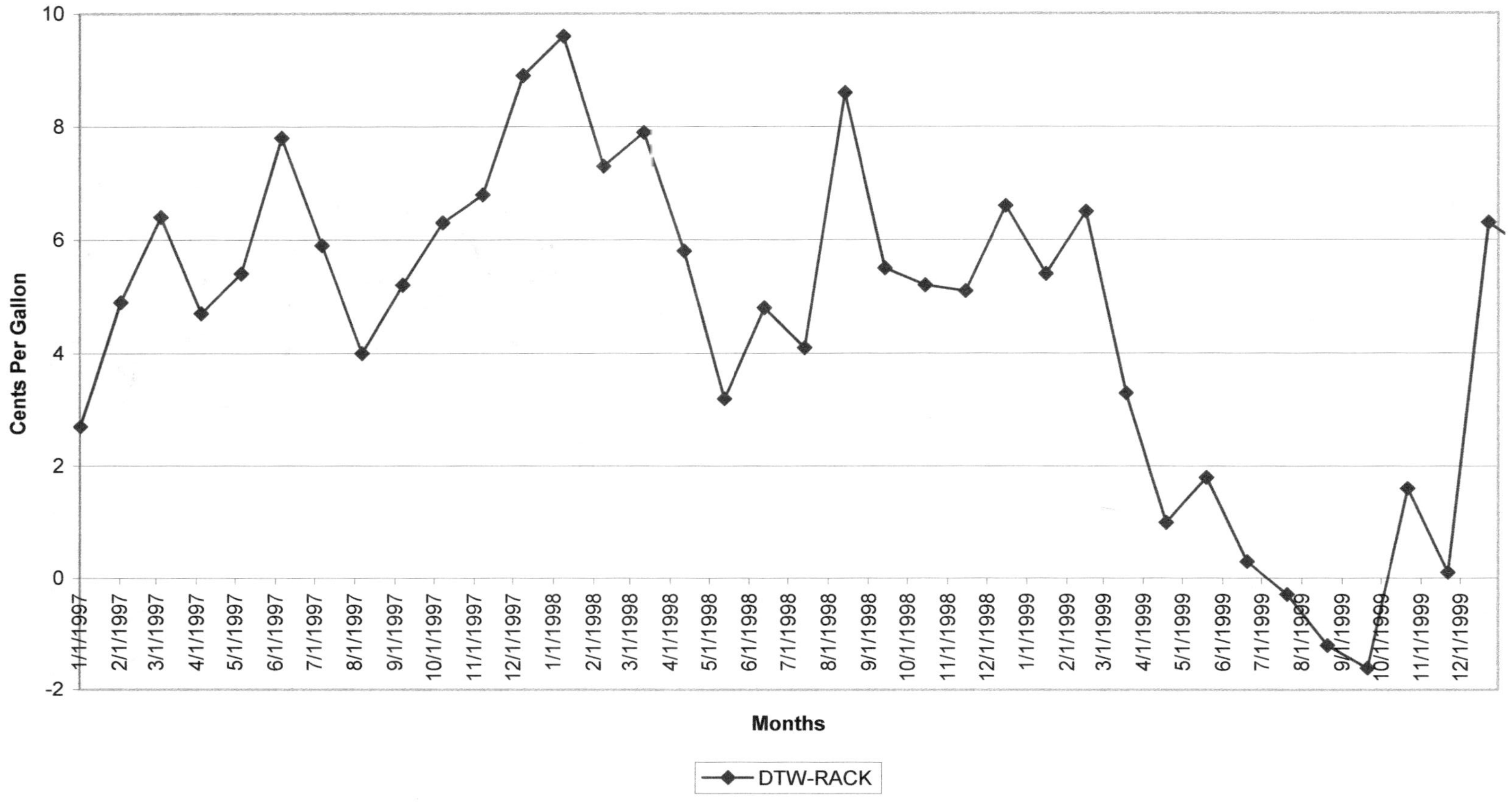

Figure A-1
Difference in Residuals of Retail Prices - Direct and Rack Supplied Stations in Louisville

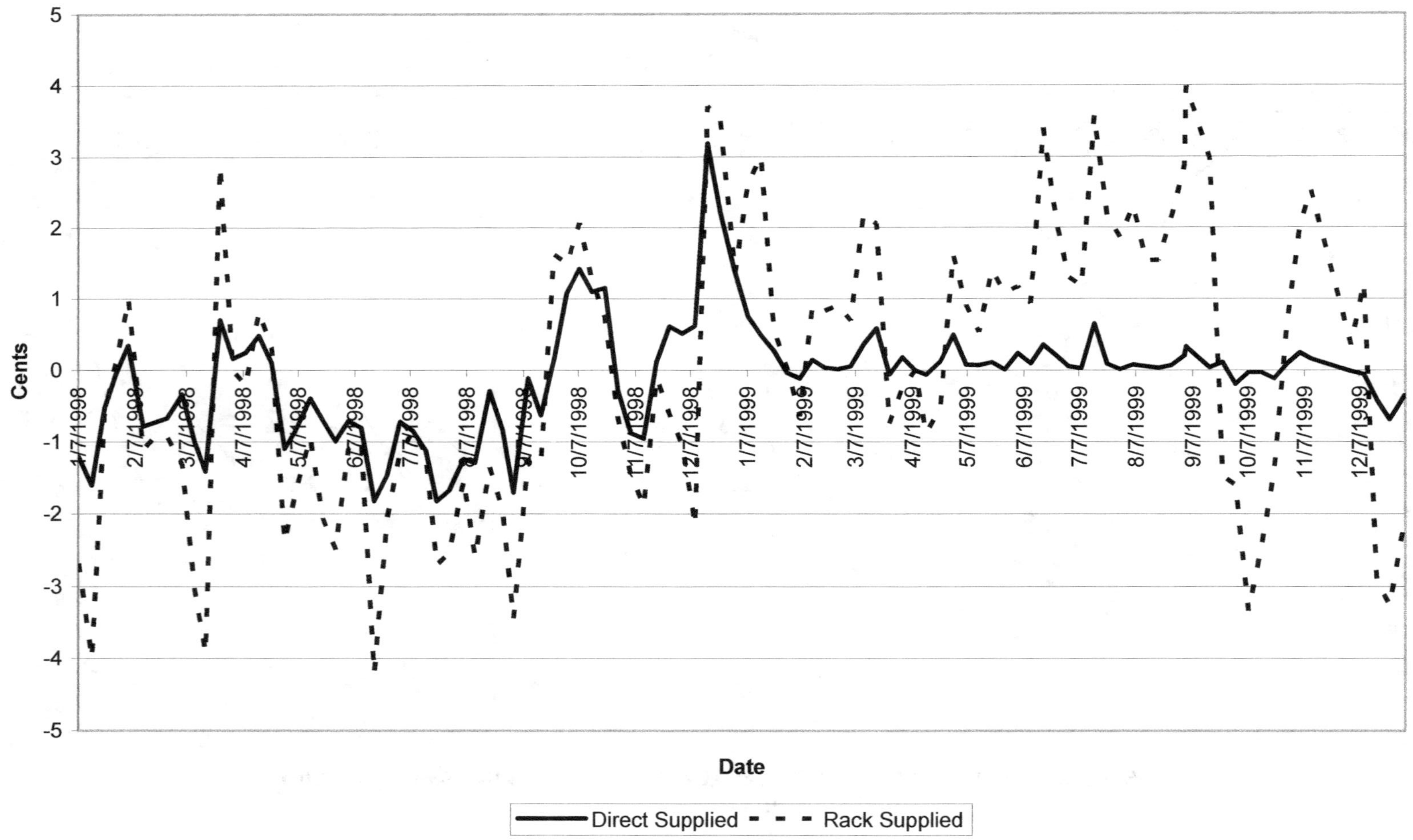

www.ingramcontent.com/pod-product-compliance
Lightning Source LLC
Chambersburg PA
CBHW081231170526
45165CB00009B/3037